Caring for Creatures

by Mary Jean Brooks

RoseDog Books

PITTSBURGH, PENNSYLVANIA 15238

RoseDog Books
585 Alpha Drive, Suite 103
Pittsburgh, PA 15238
Visit our website at *www.rosedogbookstore.com*

ISBN: 979-8-88812-394-2
eISBN: 979-8-88812-894-7

This book is dedicated to my grandchildren:
Miranda, Madeline, William, Jacob, Brooklyn
They have heard my stories over and over again.
They encouraged me to write them down to read and remember the mostly true tales of my life.
To my husband of over 50 years now, Larry, our life together has been an awesome adventure!
To my great grandchildren, I leave a legacy of love and these stories to share.

Mary J. Brooks is also author of "Faith, Family, Future" a collection of prayers, poems, and prose. She has journaled for over 45 years. This has been her walk and talk with God, helping many through times times. Mary continues to battle stage four metastatic breast cancer. Grateful for surrounding support of family and friends. Mary shared her talents and stories with too many kids to count as she worked at elementary schools for over 30 years. Thank God for the ability to write!

"All things work together for good to those who love the Lord" and are called according to his purposes - Romans 8:29

God's Creature's

God's creatures are here on earth for a very special reason.
They give such comfort, and constant caring they lavish love on those they choose, giving us a lifetime of laughter and love.
Dedicated and devoted to us even though we can be crabby and sometimes cruel.
They endow us with their unconditional faith and unwavering trust.

Through the tough moments of our lives, their tender tributes of affection carry us until we discover new hope again.
In our busy times when we take our creatures for granted, they wait patiently for us to come and seek them.
They tend to sacrifice their wants and needs for our joy, and together we can enjoy each other without fear of rejection.

God's creatures are a part of him, always steady, secure, and strong.
Waiting for us to come to him for true compassion and benevolent kindness.
People often disappoint and dissolution us, at times betraying our love and our trust.
Misunderstandings can cloud our words, and others can misjudge our actions.

The eyes of God's creatures never see wrong, their only hurt is neglect or mistreatment,
The ears of God's creatures, never take things the wrong way, they respond to the familiar gentle voice they know.
The mouths of God's creatures never say cruel harsh words only sounds of contentment and caring are heard.
The heart of God's creatures can be broken, or stop beating one day.
Yet never forgotten in his vast domain.

They embrace us with their whole heart, and grace us with their trusting souls.
God's creatures are guardian angels on earth to remember and treasure always.

Mary J. Brooks

The Farm

I love animals, especially cats. They are so cute and cuddly. We were moving to a small town, and were going to rent a farm house. My parents thought a cat would be a good idea since mice seemed to be all over on a farm. Dad let me be in charge of the new kitten, since he knew I would take good care of her. I got to hold the little ball of fluff on our four hour drive south. The kitten was mostly gray with a little white, and a cute little pink nose. On our way my siblings and I tried to think of a name. Then I heard a new song on the radio, Tammy's in love, the kitten had her name, Tammy! We arrived at the farm late that night. We couldn't see very well, but smelled some not good smells. Being we couldn't clean at that time and Mom wouldn't let us explore until the house got cleaned. We put down sleeping bags and camped out in the empty dining room. We had arrived in early summer and had lots to do helping to organize I loved the big farm house, the cozy kitchen, large dining room, living room and a small bathroom were on the first floor. We could also use the outhouse in a pinch. I was delighted to discover I got to have a room of my own, for the first time ever. The upstairs had one big bedroom for Dad and Mom, one huge dorm type room for my four younger brothers, and three tiny bedrooms for my older brother, sister, and me. My room faced the barnyard with a barn, chicken coop, grain shed, machine shed, and pastures for the cattle and sheep. I only had room for a small bed, dresser, and my own desk. It was mine and I could decorate it as I wanted. I going to turn ten soon, my favorite color was pink. I got pink walls and a pink and white graham checked bedspread and curtains. Tammy would love to sleep on my bed where she could get away from the younger boys, as they were not allowed in my room, unless I said so. All of us kids loved exploring our new surrounding. We left no stone unturned in finding a swimming hole, sneaking in the corn crib, machine shed, and barn. We watched the animals in the field and got to know their routine. The neighbors a couple miles away, had a mangy looking mutt that adopted our family. Rolly was usually full of burrs, ticks, but loveable just the same. We had fun trying to teach him tricks, and playing fetch with balls and sticks. When Rolly saw Tammy it was strange. He didn't bark, and Tammy didn't hiss. They actually liked eachother. Together they made quite a pair, running along with us kids as we enjoyed our summer freedom. We didn't have chores but the farmer who worked the farm and owned it let us kids help with haying, feeding the livestock, even riding in back of his pick up truck. Though he had no kids of his own, he liked us and got a kick out of our antics! Childhood is a carefree happy time. No time was more joyful than our year on the farm.

Thank God for Animal friends
Mary J. Brooks

Danger in Paradise

We called the beautiful valley where our farm was Shangri la after a made up place that was perfect. Yet there were dangers on the land and in the buildings. We had fun exploring every inch of this perfect place. We found a great swimming hole just beyond the creek. We older kids could go swim as long as we had a buddy. The younger kids could only go swim if Dad went. One hot day we enjoyed time in the water, but stayed a little late. We were quickly running home, when we stopped in our tracks. We heard a rattling sound. Looking around we saw a rattlesnake in the tall grass. We carefully and quickly went around the long way. I threw my towel over the snake to let Dad know it's location. We could hardly get our breath to tell Dad about the snake. He told us to stay put, and he got his shot gun. Tim went with Dad where they found my towel and the snake sunning himself on a rock. Dad shot the snake, as he couldn't let a poisionous snake near us kids. He took the rattles and dried them out. Then hung them high for us kids to see and remember to be careful! We never saw another ratteler on the land there.

Every building had some danger, and we weren't aloud in the machine shed or corn crib. The barn was one of our favorite places to play. We moved hay bails around and made forts, we swang from the rope yelling like Tarzan. We had to be careful not to go too close to the cover that moved so the farmer could throw feed down to the cattle and sheep. One rule we had to follow was to leave the bar and go home if a storm came. Lightning could start a fire.

One rainy day we were playing for an hour before we heard the storm. I was the last one out, remembering to turn off the lights and close the door tight. I started running to the house when a lightning bolt struck the ground in front of me. I could smell and feel electricity. Mom came running out thinking the bolt had hit me. I was knocked down, okay but shook up. I was thankful to be alive. From then on I had a fear of storms and always went to a safe place.

Thank God he watches over me,
Mary J. Brooks

Chubby Checkers

To get to the farm one had to drive a few miles into Iowa and turn at the little white church on the hill. You would follow the dirt road past big oak trees, huge pines, and a lots of other trees and bushes. The drive was beautiful and even us kids enjoyed the beauty. All of a sudden we burst into an opening showing the prettiest valley we had ever seen. The house was nestled in a grove of trees, and the building spread out with a large pastures for the cattle and sheep and lots of acres for us city kids to explore. There were a few neighbors near by, but no kids. The seven of us grew close because we were all we had to keep from being alone. Now I didn't mind being alone, but it was more fun to find adventures with my siblings.

We didn't see a lot of the animals as they were either in the barn or out in the pasture. The farmer did point out one of the most important animals. A huge heifer bull! He was huge, reddish brown, and had horns growing out of the top of his head. The farmer warned us not to go into his pen or pasture as he would charge and could trample us! Of course we found the bull fascinating and whenever we saw him we would go take a look. We would give him some hay and sometimes just tease him without feeding him. We named him Chubby Checkers, who was a large man who sang and invented to twist back in the 60's. One day my brother Mark and I decided to go to the neighbors, but wanted to take a shortcut through the pasture. We checked the field and didn't see the bull where he usually hung out. We thought he was in the barn, so we ran freely through the pasture. We were almost to the end when we stopped in shock. There was Chubby Checkers, looking bigger and meaner than ever. We took off for the fence barely making it over as the bull came charging at us. The bull blew smoke out his nostrils and pawed the ground, looking right at us. I could almost hear him say. I could've got you, so don't ever come in my field or tease me again! We learned our lesson! Thank You Jesus, and Chubby Checker!

Mary J. Brooks

Tomboy!

Way back when I was ten, I was called a tomboy. I loved sports and played hardest at any game or competition. I enjoyed played with my younger brothers, but I was nervous about starting a new school as kids sometimes teased me about liking "boy" games. The day before school started we were invited to a picnic for new teachers to get to know current teachers and their families. My Dad was the new History teacher, and head football coach. It's not easy being a teacher kid(TK). Other teachers and community members expected us to be smart and well behaved, just like a P.K.(preachers kid). We had to have the picnic inside, as it was pouring rain. After our lunch we went to the school gym to play games and get some energy out. I wanted to do my best and show the other kids I was a good player. I did well, and by the last game was feeling pretty good. We played pom pom pull away. I only had to break through the hands and I would win the game. I gave my all and broke through I was running so fast I couldn't stop when I reached the wall. Slam! My face smashed into the wall. I fell over with the force and saw stars. My brothers went running to get our parents. I didn't cry, but I felt like it! I toughed it out, but I felt really dumb. My nose swelled up, below my eyes colors of bruising appeared. The doctor checked me out, but other than a broken nose and black eyes, there was no head injury. Thankful for that! I went to school that first day and was asked over and over what happened to me. It was a good way to meet lots of kids. I was already known for being brave! Thank God for help.

Mary J. Brooks

Fall Fun

Fall on the farm was an amazing assortment colors as the leaves turned and started to fall. The only thing wrong with the fall was we had to leave the barn and go to school. School was okay, I really loved Music, Gym, English, and Social Studies. I didn't like Math, I didn't get it and didn't ask for help. I met some nice girls and start in talking on our old crank phone about cute boys. We had a party line we shared with our neighbor. Our ring was two long rings, the other party had two short rings and one long. After school we sstill had part of the day to run and play. We kids lived for the weekends. We would walk a mile to the mailbox at the top of alot of hills. Our walks always brought adventure. We would walk quietly not to scare our animal friends. We would see deer, raccoon, squirrels, skunk, and others. We left them alone and they left us alone.

Being my Dad was head football coach and my oldest brother was on the team, we got to go to all the home games on Friday night's. Under the big lights of the football field I found out about the game. Soon I was familiar with all the cheers and what they meant. If I didn't know something I asked my brother or my Dad. I loved watching the cheerleaders and dreamed of one day being in front of the crowd cheering. They even had a cheer song with my Dad's name in it. I proudly sang along as those that knew our family looked our way. When our team won the game we celebrated with pop and popcom. When we lost we cheered Dad up with positive feedback, and sometimes a batch of fudge. Our favorite times were Sunday night's, we had family devotions, and sing along together all nine of us. On cold, rainy, days I spent time at the desk in my room writing poems and stories. I had always loved reading, and now I could make up my own adventures. I could be anything and do anything in my story leaving my life and making up a new one. Thank God for Reading and Writing!
Mary J. Brooks

Winter Wonderland

Another great part of the farms location, was living close to some of our favorite relatives. Uncle Palmer was a Pastor and a lot of fun. Aunt Lydia was special too. Together they always had a new game to try. Our three cousins were good sports also. We spent the holidays together. Thanksgiving on the farm and Christmas at their house. Together we feasted and had fun! Although I liked playing with the boys, I wanted one of those new Barbie dolls really bad. For Christmas I was overjoyed to get a Barbie doll and Barbie paper dolls. Our family got a gift we all could enjoy, a sleek long toboggan. We quickly bundled up and almost ran to find a long hill. Snow covered the trees, the hills and made everything so pretty. We sang "Walking in the Winter Wonderland" as we found our first big hill. We were all excited to try our new present out. First Dad gave us instructions. He showed us on to lean as he leaned. He told us never to stand up while

sliding, and if he shouted "Bail Out" we needed to roll off the toboggon right away, no questions asked. There could be a tree or other obstacle in the way. We piled on first Dad, then a younger, an older, and so on until seven of us were on. Once we cleared a path, we started going faster. We would hit bumps and scream as we laughed. Our two younger brothers were tired of trudging up the hill and wanted to ride up. Dad just told them, if you don't walk up, you don't slide down. They decided to wait and watched us climb up the hill. Down we flew faster than ever. We zoomed past the boys and headed for the ditch. "Bail Out" came the shout, and we all tumbled out, laughing as cold wet snow covered our faces. "Let's do it again" we yelled. But it was getting late and time to head home. The little boys cried to have missed the fun. Yet for many winters we had lots of adventures and antics with our gift. Thank God for the gift of Fun!

Mary. J. Brooks

Mary's Little Lamb

You all know the nursery rhyme so let me start at the beginning of mine. Spring was late in coming that year. The farmer told us to keep an eye on the sheep as they were due to have their lambs early. Because it was still freezing, the mother's to be were kept in the barn, but once in awhile a stray would get out. The farmer didn't want any frozen lambs. We took our job watching the sheep seriously. I was especially excited to see the baby lambs. One night I told Dad the sheep seemed louder and more active than normal. He went out to check later and found a baby lamb frozen to the ground. It was too late for that one, but Dad called the farmer and us older kids went out to the barn to watch the lambs being born. We promised to stay out of the way. This was quite an eye opening experience for us city kids! It was exciting to see the new births, and those babies were the cutest things you've ever seen after they were cleaned up. One of the sheep had twins. One was a yellowish color and one was a chocolate color.

Something was wrong though, the mother sheep would not feed the little chocolate one. We had named them Lemon Drop and Chocolate Drop. The farmer explained that ewe's (Mom sheep) rejected the runt sometimes. I begged and pleaded to take the little lamb into the house to keep him warm and try to feed him. We all wanted to keep him alive. My siblings helped too. All night long we used an eye dropper to get some of his mom's milk into this little guy. It was funny watching him try to suck on the eyedropper. The next day I was mostly left to feed the lamb, and he had the hang of getting some milk in him.. I did take time out to see all the new babies and help name them. Licorice, Snowball, Cotton, and so on. I was thankful we were on spring break and I could spend time with my lamb. By the time we went back to school Chocolate Drop was now named Sooty and be was drinking out of a baby bottle. It started warming up and the snow was melting when we got a picture of some of us with the lambs. I held my Sooty of course. Though his fleece was not as white as snow, he started following me, Mary, everywhere I would go. He couldn't follow me to school on the bus or in the car though. He was always waiting for me when I returned home. The cutest, cuddlest ball of fluff you ever saw! I loved my lamb.

Thank God for Little Lambs!

Mary J. Brooks

Sooty and Splash

Shortly after Sooty was hearty enough to join the other sheep and lambs outside. Dad bought a calf, he was a Holstein. They are white and black cows. This little guy looked like he was splashed with black paint. That's how he got his name. Sooty wasn't being accepted by the other animals, but Splash took to him right away. Together they did everything, the farmer even made a stall for the two of them. They were happiest together. The lambs had been born March 1st, and Splash shortly after. By May both Sooty and Splash were growing fast. Spring Fever got into two of my little brothers and they showed the lamb and calf how to butt heads. They also started butting others. They were gentle with me, but sometimes rough on others when they butted.

One day they went crazy! Mom was outside hanging up clothes. When they saw her bending over the clothes basket they went running for her and butted her. She fell on her fanny, and saw them getting ready to come at her again. She barely got to the outside basement door when the butted that. She waited until she didn't see them and was able to get to the kitchen before they got on the porch and butted the door!

Later after school Dad didn't have practice that day, so we rode home with him. We got to where he parked and both Sooty and Splash can running at the car, butting the doors. We were trapped. Dad had an idea. He told Jon to run to the barn, and when the crazy animals followed him, the rest of us would run to the house. Jon was really fast and got to the barn safely as we got to the house.

After awhile Jon was able to get to the house too. That afternoon we stayed inside while the two animals butted each other outside to entertain themselves and us. Maybe it was the full moon or maybe they were bored, we never knew why they were so wild and crazy that day.

Mary J. Brooks

Tootsies and Bessie

One day our landlord brought two short horned cows to the farm. Short horns are good milker's and beef cattle. Milt had bought them for a bargain price. They both were producing milk after having calves. They would be uncomfortable until they dried out. Milt told us to just leave them be. That was hard to do as they both started bellowing when he left. The kids saw them and helped name them Toosie and Bessie. Even if they were not ours, every animal got a name. As the day went on the noise got worse. Finally I told my wife I was going to milk those cow and quiet them up. I had watched Milt and copied him. I moved slowly and talked to them softly. Tootsie looked at me strangely but seemed to accept my inexperience. I warmed up my hands by rubbing them. I didn't get much milk at first. Before long I had a pailful. I proudly showed my wife, left the milk with her and went back out to take care of Bessie. She seemed a little more upset stamping her feet and giving me a dirty look. I squirted some milk at our cat Tammy, who loved to hang out in the barn. The next day Milt came back to do his chores and wondered why the cows were so quiet. I told him what I did and he turned white as a sheet. He told. me I could have gotten killed, being a stranger to the cows. He said it was natural for them to dry up and would have been okay in a few days. From then on when they saw me they came over and let me scratch their ears. They liked this city guy who thought chocolate milk came from brown cows. Praise God for nice cows!

Grandpa Duck/Fred Kuss

Chicks Everywhere!

My Dad had the great idea of ordering some baby chicks from the seed catalog he was looking at as he planned his garden. Young fryers were cheap, and didn't take long to raise. Their feed was cheaper than hen chicks who laid eggs and took more work to raise. There was alot of grass and bugs on the farm for the chickens to eat too. Our farmer friend said we could use the empty chicken coop, which just needed to be cleaned out. Dad got the building ready, and even bought a heat lamp to keep the chicks warm as Spring nights could get cold. Then he ordered one hundred fryer chicks, and his mouth watered thinking of fried chicken in a few months. Dad wasn't sure how those little chick would come, or exactly when, but the coop was ready for them. One bright sunny morning, we were all at school except toddler, David. Mom saw the rural mailman drive down by the house. This was unusual as we always had to walk to get the mail. The mailman gave Mom a long box. She heard the peeping noises right away and was taken by surprise to see all those tiny yellow baby chicks in the box. They were contained in a box with a lid and holes for air. How much trouble would they be to keep them in the kitchen until Dad came home in a few hours. It was cool outside anyway and Mom thought it be better to keep them in the house. She put them by the stove and did her work. Everything was going great. The chicks peeping away in their box. Then Mom wondered if the chicks were getting enough air and being a Mom, she thought maybe she should feed them. She took off the cover and put some oatmeal and water in the box. She took three year old David upstairs as she made some beds and got some clothes to wash. Awhile later later they came back downstairs and was shocked to see those little chicks everywhere. David laughed and tried to catch them while Mom scooped them up and put them back in the box. They got out just as fast as she put them in. Then she found a box with higher sides so the baby chicks couldn't get out. By the time she got them contained the floor was a mess of bird droppings, water, and oatmeal. It took Mom the rest of the day as Dave napped to get her kitchen back in order. As we heard Mom's story, we couldn't help laughing over the thought of Mom trying to capture all those chicks with Dave being no help at all. Right after Dad took the chicks out to their new home in the chicken coop where they belonged.

Thank God for Chickens and Coops!

Mary J. Brooks

The Long Walk Home

Summer was coming and we were excited for school to end and have the whole summer to enjoy our freedom on the farm. We didn't usually ride the school bus, but when my Dad was busy coach in football in the fall and track in the spring we sometimes needed to ride the bus. We were six miles from school. The bus drove over the border into Iowa and then down the long driveway to drop us off. We were the last kids to be dropped off. We had two days of school left on that warm June 1st day. Tim was with Dad at a track meet, Jon and Dave were at home. We got to the Iowa border and the bus stopped. The driver told us we had to walk from there, as the bus could no longer go into Iowa due to a new rule that had just gone into effect. The four of us got off the bus and started the long walk home, my older sister,

my two younger brothers and me. We girls helped our brothers by playing games and running races as we reached the church and our driveway two miles later. By the time we reached the house over an hour later, our Mom was frantic. She had called the school and found out what happened. No one had told her or Dad about the new rule. She tried to call Dad but the track team was away. She called our friend Milt, the farmer who came with the pick up truck just as we got home. After some cookies and lemonade the boys and I were ready to ride in the back of the pick up, which was our of our favorite thrills. We rode by the fields checking on the cattle and sheep. We loved the feeling of speed as the wind blew our hair and onto our hot faces. This was a nice treat after our long walk home. Later that night we found out really sad news. We would have to leave the farm and find a house in town because of the new bus rule. We were crushed thinking of having to leave the farm and our animals. Milt said we could always visit the animals, and he would get some renters to care for his livestock and our pets. After I cried that night, I felt better when Dad told us to enjoy the last months on the farm. Mom and he started planning a big family reunion. After we moved the end of July, he promised would we would take a trip to California, visit our grandparents and go to Disneyland.

Thankful for promises kept!
Mary J. Brooks

Saying Goodbye

Our last two months on the farm were the best ever. We built forts, went fishing, swimming, hiking, and used our minds to make up stories we acted out. We spent lots of time with Sooty, Splash, Tammy and Rolly. We gave Chubby Checkers lots extra treats and hung out by his pasture watching him in awe. We got ready for the big family reunion that we were hosting on the farm. Our uncles, aunts, cousins, grandparents, extended family were coming to stay. Some would be there just a day, others would be there four days. We gathered together, played games, and had relays. Water balloon toss, egg race, funny sack race, and three legged races. We play card games, and our favorite "PIT" in the evening. We had sing alongs and skits by the campfire. Many funny and scary stories were told, and our potluck picnics were the best! Our cousins had all been jealous of our farm life, and now they felt bad we were moving. We were happy to share our fun, our animals, and our beautiful outdoor area with all! Our relative loved our animals and their antics. Thankfully our calf and lamb no longer butted people, just each other. We had yummy fried chicken on Sunday from the chickens Dad had bought. Thankfully they were butchered elsewhere. We had a special outdoor church service with my two Uncles presiding. One could feel the presence of God surrounding us. We celebrated my brother Mark and my birthday. There was a huge cake, and lots of presents!

After the reunion it was time to start packing to move to town. Dad and Mom had found us a big house two blocks from the new town swimming pool. I hated to leave my own room, and would have to share with my sister again. There were so many things we were sad to leave behind. We gave our neighbor Tammy our cat, as Rolly the dog, would be lost without his best friend. We had to say goodbye to Splash and my beloved Sooty. Milt, the farmer promised to take care of them, and said we could visit. Our family had grown close, as we learned to help and depend on each other out on the farm away from others. The farm had been more than just a place to live, it was a time of pure joy. The sweet memory of that year will remain in my heart always.

Thank God for farm memories!
Mary J. Brooks

California, Here We Come!

The last day of July we quickly moved from the farm into town. We packed up the black and white station wagon, which we called the skunk. We didn't organize, unpack, or even clean. We left early Aug. 1st for our vacation to California. We would visit my Dad's parents, go to Disneyland, and see a few of Mom's cousin. After hours in the old skunk, it smelled sweaty, and we six kids were bored. We didn't complain though, we wouldn't dare! We played the alphabet game, I spy, license plates game, sang songs, and made up stories to pass the time. By the time we reached the Black Hills, we were ready for a break. Mount Rushmore was amazing. The huge Buffalo we saw out the car window were unbelievably huge. We stopped at historical sights too as our Dad was a History teacher. We went to Yellowstone National Park in Wyoming. We saw the signs right away. "Do Not Feed The Bears". Shortly after we saw cars stopped and people were feeding those wild bears. We camped there one night, saw the geysers and Old Faithful erupt. We also saw mountain goats, bobcat, skunk, raccoon, and by the time we left the park we had counted 32 bears. They looked cute and cuddly but they were wild animals and we obeyed the signs. Feeding the bears would cause them to not hunt for their food, which would hurt them eventually.

In Buffalo Wyoming our car broke down. We got to stay at a beautiful campground for two weeks. We kids were in heaven! There was a swimming pool, playground, and kids to play with our ages. We hiked and biked, played ball, and games. It cost our poor parents alot, but we didn't have to think about that.

Once the car was fixed we got through the mountains, beautiful yet scary with soaring heights. Then through the hot, scorching desert with no air conditioning as the sun beat down on our black car! We finally reached California, sweaty, tired, crabby, and overheated. Almost to our grandparents house. Mom told us not to ask for anything, just sit nice and listen. Grandpa Kuss knew better. He told us kids to look out in the back yard. We saw the most beautiful sight, a big new above ground swimming pool. We looked at each other afraid to move until Grandpa said, "Last one in is a rotten egg!" You never saw kids change clothes to swim suits so fast! After an hour of swimming, Grandma came out with homemade cookies and lemonade! All those day hours in the car had been worth it! We got to know these far away grandparents too, and it was great to know them and their love. Thank God for Grandparents!

Mary J Brooks

Geronimo

We had the best, bustling, busy time while in California. We had to head back to settle in our house and get ready for school to start. We needed to see the Grand Canyon first. We got there around one and the native American guide told us about the legend of Geronimo. He was the Apache leader in the area. He was greatly feared and respected. Mexican's and American's alike tried to take over the land his tribe lived on. Geronimo had fierce courage, and his actions were driven by revenge. He was credited with supernatural powers, heal the sick, cause storms to strike, and have premonitions that came true.

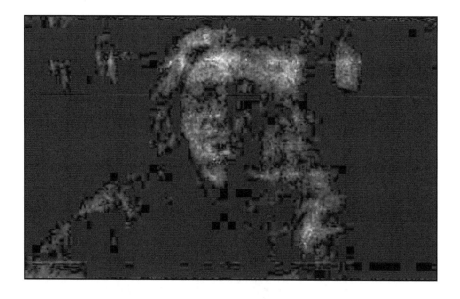

The guide told Dad we could take the last six mules down to where they say Geronimo discovered buried treasure and others tried to steal it. Being it was getting late us kids could go for free. The guide warned us to be back up from the canyon before sunset, as those that had betrayed Geronimo would come back to wander and ask for forgiveness from Geronimo. It was now two in the afternoon we had until six to explore. Dad with Danny on the first mule led the way, then Tim, Marti, Me, Mark, and last Mom and Jonny. It was a little scary, but very beautiful along the trail. After two hours we headed back. This time the mules were stubborn. The mule Mom and Jonny were on refused to go, we tried everything and then dad found some sweet clover and held it far enough for the mule to go after it. Finally we were almost back and darkness was reaching to the canyon. We thought we heard whispering, and then it was louder, "Geromino, Geromino". First Dad and Dan made it, then Tim, Marti, Mom and Jon. Mark and I felt hands trying to get us, pulling our legs. "Geronimo, GEROMINO!" Pulling our legs, pulling our legs, (dramatic pause) just like I'm pulling yours! We did go to the Grand Canyon and learn about Geromino but the rest was a fictional story made up by our Dad, and over time the story is a favorite campfire story! We made it back to Minnesota in time to get settled before school began. Thank God for Great memories and great stories.

Fred Kuss/Mary Brooks

In Town and Around

We got settled in town, and though we missed the farm there were advantages. We had lots of kids near by to play with and befriend. The house just across the street had an empty lot where we discovered was the play lot for kids. After supper we would gather and play games. Annie, Annie Over, Red light, Green light, Starlight Moonlight hope to see the ghost tonight. I put my all in each game, as did my brothers. Being coaches kids we were competitive. One night while playing to win, I slipped on the grass and felt a sharp object in my knee. I went home bleeding, and Dad took me down out the back of our house where the doctor had an office. It was painful getting glass out of my knee, and seven stiches were put in also. The next day we went through the lot and cleaned any sharp object out. We then did that everyday before we played. In town we could ride bikes every-where. The streets were paved and not gravel. My bike was too small now and went to my younger brothers. I shared with my sister, until I could get a bigger bike. One day my brother Mark and I saw a nice looking boys English racer laying on the sidewalk. A few days later we saw it still there. We told Dad about it, he said to ask around. Then if no one claimed it we could. No one claimed it, and we went and got it. I got on to try it out, and it rode like a dream! As we went downhill towards home, I tried the brakes, and they didn't work. I thought quick how do I stop this thing? I drove on the grass to slow down and put my feet down to stop. I couldn't reach the ground so hopped off in one piece. From then on I had the bike to myself and was careful to think about how to slow down and stop. Going up a hill always worked or riding into tall grass. It was a little dangerous, but always an adventure. That summer Dad and Mom took us four older kids to the New York World's Fair and to Washington D.C. The World's Fair was great. It was like traveling through each county. We saw the Statue of Liberty from the ferry, that brought a tear to my eye. New York City was too loud and crowded for us, we didn't stay long. We did liked seeing the Liberty Bell and the history everywhere. Washington DC. was full of beauty and history too. The Capital, the White House, Lincoln Memorial, Jefferson Memorial, Washington Monument, Mount Vernon, Arlington Cemetary, Gettysburg. We saw the history we had read about and Dad filled us with more as he told us back stories and adventures of our country's past. My favorite part was going to Cape Cod and swimming in the Atlantic Ocean. Time flew by on the was home we went through Buffalo, New York and the car got overheated. Buffalo named towns were unlucky for us we decided. We got back and took full advantage of our family pass for the town swimming pool. I did manage to hit me head on the cement pool trying to attempt a back dive. The lifeguard took me home, once again the doctor saw me and and I had a slight concussion. That didn't keep me down for long. Between all of us seven kids we got to know the doctor well. We lived in town three more years. Our grandparents came to visit us, Grandpa Kuss encouraged me keep diving. He thought I was pretty great. Living in a small town where your Dad was a teacher wasn't the greatest part. Other teachers and people thought we should be the best at everything. Especially if your siblings were smart and special, and you didn't feel that way. I was glad to leave the small town and start over in a new area.

Thank God for Doctor's!

Mary J. Brooks

A New Start

After four years in a small town, we headed back to the city and sub-urbs of Minneapolis. You might ask if I ever went back to the farm to visit. No I didn't, seeing another family there would've broke my heart. Maybe my lamb wouldn't remember me either. I wanted to re-member our perfect year there and not spoil the memory with real life. Dad had gotten a job teaching summer school so there was no time to find a place to live. The Grandpa and Grandma opened their little two bedroom house to our large family. It was crowded and noisy. I found my refuge in the library two blocks away. Also took a class of English and Drama that I loved. There was a nice house across from the school where I met some nice girls. That didn't work out. Then another larger new house across from a different school became available. I still had to share a room with my sister, but the house was beautiful. It had two fireplaces, a large living room, dining, room, and family room. The little boys would take the bus to the Elementary School, but my sister, me, and one brother could walk to school. There was a big empty field across the street which was perfect for playing football and baseball. I loved playing football with my brothers, and there friends. I was pretty tough, so they called me brickwall. Hitting me, or when I was tackling someone I felt like a brickwall. The day before schools started we were playing. I got the ball and made the touchdown, even though one of the boys talked me. My body went one way and my knee went another. I had to see a doctor as my knee was dislocated. The doctor put a long needle in my knee and drained the fluids, pulled my knee back into the joint(ouch) wrapped it up and gave me crutches to use for six weeks. The first day of school there was knowing no one, but meeting and making new friends due to my injury. The gals I met formed quite a group of girls about a dozen of us. We weren't the popular girls, we were more geeks. We had the most fun and were inclusive to anyone.

I was the main organizer and planner for school events, parties, and events beyond school. We had lots of school spirit, going to games and dressing up to fit the theme of the week. For "Clean Up Centennial", we dressed as maids, and cleaning ladies. We had our crushes, shared our life's and loves. I am still friends with many of these silly, sweet, special girls to this day.

There were three of us best friends. I can't share alot of our secrets, but one story shows our adventurous spirit. We stayed over night at our one friends house on a lake. We would sneak out and walk on the gravel road, when a car came we would drop down in a ditch and remain unseen. One night as we were getting up from our hiding places, we heard a strange noise. It was a whirring sound and pretty loud. We walked towards the sound, and then saw bright lights. We dropped down to hide as something wooshed over our heads. We peeked between the trees and saw a large round indentation in an open area with woods all around. We believed it was a UFO of some kind, and never shared this with the other girls. We never went to that area again. We called ourselves the three musketeers because we always stuck together, "all for one, and one for all" and we always had a ball! Thank God for new friends!

Mary J. Brooks

Careful When Camping

I have always enjoyed camping and I thought some of my friends should try it too. My friend lived on a lake across the lake was some uninhabited land that we have seen people camp on. We decided to give it a try. There was no electricity, just a porta potty workers used. There were us four gals and our four guys. We each had a tent to share, boys in one and girls in the other. We had lanterns and cook stoves too. We set up in a fairly flat piece of land. We explored, ate, drank, played games, and told scary stories around the campfire. Then the hungry mosquitoes came out and drove us into our tents. We could her them buzzing outside, the screen. No one got much sleep, and we decided to pull up stakes and go back to the apartment where we girls lived. As we were putting things away one guy found a wood tick on him. Then we all started feeling them crawling on us. Some had them in them dining on their blood. One guy had a total of 18 on him. Most of us had two or three we found, but we still felt a crawling sensation and it was creepy. From that day on we called the land, "Wood Tick Hill", and never went back there again.

My fiance and I, my good friend and her fiance, did alot of things together. We always tended to find adventure. We decided to go north of Duluth to visit my fiance's brother who was stationed there in the army. We found a nice campground nearby and were prepared with deep woods off, bug spray! The campground manager warned us to keep our food in the trunk and not leave any garbage around, there were bears in the area. We got set up, and it started drizzling. My friends fiance decided to light the lantern in the tent unknown to us. A large flame appeared and we quickly threw a blanket over the fire in the lantern. That was a close one! We knew better then to light a lantern in a tent but he didn't.

The next day we visited my fiance's brother, went sightseeing and hiking. After supper, we went to the dump. We were told the bears hung out there around sunset. Sure enough there were a couple of bears who came to look for food. We heard there was one named Scarface, who was scary looking, always looking for a fight. All of a sudden, he was there and he was huge. He saw us in the car and climbed on the truck trying to get at the food. We were scared and drove slowly trying to get him off the car, but he just snarled at us through the glass. We waited till another bear came, and Scarface went off the car to get him. We took off like a Shot! That was way too close for comfort! Later that night when two of us were sleeping, my fiance and friend heard something very large walking around near by. They looked out, it wasn't a bear, it was a huge moose on the road. They stayed very quiet and the moose finally left. That was wise on their part. No one wants to be trambled by a giant moose! Thank God for watching over us!

Mary J. Brooks

Kitty's

Once we moved into the our ownhouse, we could finally have a pet again. How I loved having a kitty again. Jody was black and white, soft and sweet. I didn't like leaving her when I went to school. Jody loved the field where we played football. She would find mice, chase squirrels, and enjoy her freedom. She would always be back shortly after I got home from school. It seemed she knew when I was home. She would follow me, sleep with me, and loved the petting I lavished on her. We loved playing together, ribbons, yarn, and string were her favorite thing. She would hide out from my brothers in our room. Yet she liked playing a little rough with the boys. She still had her claws, so they had to be careful. She never scratched me though. We lived on a pretty busy road, so when Jody took off I got nervous about her crossing that street. We had Jody for over a year when the unimaginable happened. She was hit by a car. I had just come home and saw a car stop and a man pick her up and throw our cat in our yard. I was heartbroken to find her dead. I thought it was mean for the person to throw her, she might have been alive. At least she wasn't driven over again and again. We dug a hole in the back yard, wrapped her in a blanket and had a short funeral for Jody. She had been my best friend and I missed her very much.

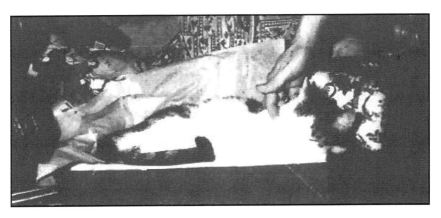

Then came Tuffy, a cute gray and white kitten. We got her in late summer and brought her to our last camp out of the year at Lake Independence. I warned my brothers to make sure to zip the door shut tight when they went out. I went to swim with friends, while they finished changing. Off they went leaving the tent unzipped. When we got back I was mad at the boys for not zipping the tent. I was upset that little tiny Tuffy was missing. We looked and called, other campers came to search too. I thought I heard something. I walked towards the sound and there she was cuddled up in leaves. I didn't leave her the rest of the time camping. We had decided to keep Tuffy indoors because of what happened to Jody. One cool fall day no one realized she had gotten out. Mom was in a hurry to get to her church meeting and backed out. Tuffy had been hiding on the warm tire and she ran her over. Poor Mom felt so bad. We all were sad, but decided to go without a pet for awhile. Our hearts needed to get over the hurt of loss. Thank God for mending hearts.

Mary Jean Brooks

The Dirty Rat

When we first moved from our little house in Robbinsdale, we missed the big shade trees and the animals that lived in them. The city of Maple Grove where we now lived planted trees on the boulevard of every house. Being we were on the corner we got two trees, they were small but they would grow. Everything around the new area of houses was was pretty bare. Across the street just behind a row of houses was a large field. We lived near the cities, but we had the feel of the country. We had neighbors near by we met and liked. Two doors down the people had a little weiner dog named Dolly. Our kids got to know her real well, and she would come over to visit and play. One day as we were outside Dolly had just come over when my phone rang. I ran in to answer it and could still see the kids. I saw the kids follow the dog to the side of the house and Dolly started barking loudly which was unusual. I quick got off the phone to see what the kids we up too.

There in our window well was the biggest rat you ever saw and my kids were laughing and trying to pet that dirty rat! Dolly was barking and keeping them away. The rat had his teeth bared ready to bite. I quickly brought the kids in the house and told them to stay there. I didn't want that rat around the kids, the dog, or our house. I went a got a shovel, closed my eyes a hit the rat striking it until it didn't move anymore. I scooped up the rat and threw him far into the field. I talked to the kids about staying away from animals they didn't know. We took Dolly home, and I told my neighbor how Dolly had saved them from getting bit. I was very grateful. When my husband got home, he heard all about my scary experience with a sewer rat.

The next day was Saturday and we went to visit some of my husband's relatives out of town. As the day wore on I noticed something was off with Matt, my oldest child. He was unlike himself, overly crappy and quiet. I asked him if he felt okay several times. He had a little fever starting, so we headed home. He couldn't get his shirt off and seemed in pain. I helped him and his right shoulder had a huge red blister that looked like he had been burned. I called the doctor and brought Matt into the emergency room. They took him away and I couldn't follow right away. The medical staff started asking me all these questions, what happened, what did we do, etc. I had no idea what was going on I felt like an abuser, but I know they have to check everything out. I finally got to be with Matt and while we waited the blister and redness started spreading. Test showed that he had a staff infection, which can be very serious. They started him on antibiotics and he stayed the night in the hospital. Of course I stayed right there with my little three year old, praying for his healing. It was surprising how calm I stayed. Getting all frightened and upset would've only upset Matt. My husband thought maybe the rat scratched our son, and I mentioned that to the doctor. We will never know what caused the infection. We were thankful Matt got better quickly and was able to go home. We never saw a rat like that in all the years we have lived in the area. Thank God for Medicine, and Prayers!

Mary J. Brooks

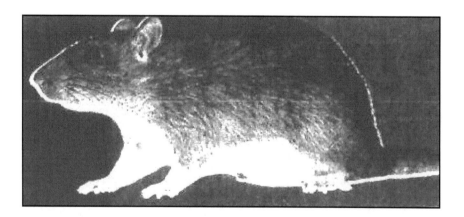

Mac and Dawn: Our Mallard Ducks

We had lived in our house about five years when the ducks first came. Our area just had small trees, and run off areas we called ponds. As grass got planted amd trees grew the ducks and geese came to enjoy the nearby ponds. We would walk to the ponds with our old bread and feed the ducks and geese. We loved seeing the babies in the spring after they hatched, they were so cute. The Mama ducks weren't so glad to see those noisy kids. They learned to be quiet so we could watch them.

Our neighbor behind us gave us his crab tree, which he didn't like. My husband planted it in front of our kitchen window. There he hung bird feeders where we could watch the different birds come and enjoy the seeds. One day my twins came running in getting my full attention as they shouted, ""Mom, we have ducks!" There under the tree was a male drake, and a female hen, They were eating the seeds that the birds had dropped. I thought they would leave and that would be the end, but the ducks continued to show up all summer. I must say we missed watching them when they left. The next year, they were back on the first nice day after our long Minnesota winter. The kids named them Mac and Dawn as they were our ducks now. Flakey watched them out the window, but we made sure he didn't get out to bother them. The kids stayed far away to quietly watch the ducks and not scare them. As they left for the South, the kids knew they would be back.

Sure enough they came back year after year, each spring and summer they fed under our tree. Mac would let Dawn eat first, and then he would eat. Other ducks would come, but Mac and Dawn chased them out of their territory. We never saw any baby duck eggs, or ducklings. They nested nearer the water most likely. Our kids, teens, and then grandkids enjoyed watching the ducks. We knew the first ducks were gone, but we called the ducks kids, and grandkids,

Mac and Dawn also. My husband bought special seed for the ducks and they loved it! The year my daughter and her husband came to live with us with their two loud, nosy, dogs, the ducks came, but left in a few days, Mac and Dawn did not like these dogs. The dogs barked at them and would try to chase them. The dogs were gone by the next year, and the ducks came back. They only stayed a couple days and left. From then on we got a couple ducks here and there, but Mac and Dawn found another quiet place to eat and rest. We had enjoyed them for years, and they found a safe haven with us for years. Thank God for Ducks!

Mary J. Brooks

Flakey Finds A Home

I had been wanting to get a kitten again for years, but with three active, adventurous kids I wasn't sure we should add one to our busy household. The kids kept begging and promised to be gentle and helpful if we got a kitten. I saw an ad for free kittens, so decided to go and look. I saw the one I wanted right away. He was a combination of gray, white, black, and even a little brown and most important he liked to snuggle. He was ready to leave as he was growing fast. There had been four other kittens at first. Now weeks later there was only two kittens left. People came, he was picked up petted and put down. He liked the attention and was lonely when the people left. The kids grandparents would pick up the kitten. The strange other people picked him up and took him out into the cold, bright world. He was put into a small warm room there was food and water, but he was alone. He had everything he needed except someone to care for him and love him. Where was his new home and new family? The family had been gone and now came home to surprise the kids. The kitten heard strange noises which made him nervous. There were excited voices and lots of laughing. The kitten meowed over, and over again. The little girl heard him and the kids ran down to see what was making the noise. Finally the door opened someone soft and tender picked up the kitten. Then was he handed to a gentle child. The girl held the kitten close, petting him gently. Then a loud, rough little boy picked up the kitten. Then a quiet boy, who petted him softly. Then the first person took him took him in her arms for safety. She who showed him such tenderness and love he knew he had found his place. He knew he had found his home. He was excited now and purred with contentment.

The little girl called him "Snowflake". The kids all played with him and petted him, but his safe haven was being held by the Mom of the house. She protected him from any rough play. Mom loved that the kids were so nice, kind, and loving to the kitten. She watched them dangle string and yarn as the kitten chased. The kitten would chase his tail, hide inside of paper bags, pounce on the bed as someone moved there feet. They all laughed and enjoyed this flakey kitten. "You aren't Snowflake, you are Flakey!" She said. It was decided that name, Flakey fit the kitten perfectly, and so did the kitten fit into this busy, bustling, family. A new member given much attention and much love made for one happy kitten!

Thank God for Family!

Mary J. Brooks

Flakey and the Kids

Flakey loved his new home and his new person they called Mom. He now needed to get used to the three kids that lived in the home too. He was getting used to the guy they called Dad. Dad wasn't around alot but he was kind and made sure the kids were careful with Flakey. The cat knew the kids were a special part of the family so he would need to get used to their noise and activity. The little girl was soft and gentle, petting Flakey and playing with him. Her name was Becky, and Flakey loved the ribbons and yarn Becky left out for him in her room. He chased them and batted his paws at them. Becky also had long silky hair she would dangle for him to play with as it hung in his face. He didn't understand why she got upset when he woke her at night playing with her hair. There were two boys in the family too. One was kind of rough and tough. His name was Brad and be had lots of energy and created lots of noise. The boy always wanted to hold Flakey even when the cat wanted to go his own way. He would play a little rougher, but would get a little sadder at times. Then Flakey would lay on Brad's chest and make him feel better. Flakey got used to Brad's roughness and enjoyed playing with him. Brad showered lots of love and attention on the cat. The other boy was quiet and calm, his name was Matt. Matt was a good kid to hang around with, nice and calm. Matt showed the cat how to play hockey with the magnet letters on the door. Flakey would wake the family up at night playing with these letters. Then Flakey would get tired and go from bed to bed sleeping wherever and with whoever he wanted.

One night Flakey was sleeping with Matt when the boy got sick. Matt had thrown up on the cat, and the cat didn't like it. Dad had to put Flakey in the laundry tub and wash him off, which the cat didn't like at all. Mom took care of the boy, but the cat wished for her! She did dry Flakey off and wrap him in warm towel. The cat didn't like his bath but he was curious about water. The kids would turn on the sink, the cat would jump up and drink. It was a silly sight to see! The kids did strange things to the cat. Becky would dress him in her doll clothes and put him in her buggy for a walk. Brad would throw a ball and chase the cat as he chased the ball. Matt would put him out in the snow at first snowfall. The cat would run in the house shaking his wet paws off. Flakey never complained or scratched, Mom always rescued him before the kids got carried away. Flakey loved his family and was happy to share his life with the three kids who loved him. The family kept him safely inside for his own good. Thank God for Kids and Cats!

Mary J. Brooks

Flakey Finds A Friend

After losing many cats to the outside world. The family decided to have Flakey be an inside cat. As an independent, curious cat Flakey didn't always like being stuck inside. When the neighbors next door got a puppy, the kids who lived with Flakey were very excited. They started going over and playing with the cute little puppy. Her name was Sammy or Sam for short. Flakey was a little upset that his kids were giving attention and love to someone else. He watched as his kids played out front with the puppy, and then the kids walked this tail wagging, sometimes barking little dog. Though Flakey didn't always like the kids bothering him, he didn't want them playing with any other animal. The kids decided that Flakey should meet Sammy, so they brought her to the screen door in the kitchen where they could see each other up close. The dog wagged his tail excitedly, but Flakey just sat and stared at her. When Sammy came closer, Flakey hissed and arched his back. That is cat language for back off or I'll attack. Cats and dogs don't like to share their people unless the start out sharing as babies. Sometimes they get used to each other over time. The kids kept trying to get Flakey and Sammy to be friends. They liked Sam, but they loved Flakey. Anytime Sammy would get loose he would run over to find the kids and the cat. Finally Flakey got used to Sammy, and his kids lavished enough love on Flakey so he wasn't jealous anymore. Then there was Tom cat, the cat across the street that Flakey would see running around the neighborhood. They would stare at each other, but not get to close. Cats think they own their people and their house. They were independent and interested, but not friendly.

My brother Tim needed a place to stay for a couple weeks and brought his cat Puff with him. Flakey thought the other cat was going to stay. He was upset that his house had to be shared. Flakey didn't like sharing one bit. He was used to things his way. The people tried to keep the cats separated. Puff wanted to be friends, and Flakey wanted him gone. Flakey sulked and ignored, Puff as he rubbed against Flakey and followed him throughout the house. Flakey started getting used to Puff and they finally became friends and had fun playing together. Then it was time for Tim and Puff to leave. Flakey looked all over for Puff, he smelled everywhere. Where was his friend? Flakey missed the cat rubbing and purring beside him. Flakey was curious now about other cats. He would sneak out and join Tom cat on his nightly rounds. They were a team, now that he learned about being a friend and trusting one another.

Yet, he always went back home to be with the family he loved, and who loved him and lavished attention on Flakey the cat. Thank God for all creatures!

Mary J. Brooks

Flakey Goes For A Ride

Flakey the cat, loved his daily routine. Breakfast, get petted, nap, snack, bathroom, nap, lunch, nap, and so on. Cats can sleep up to 20 hours a day. Flakey didn't like when his daily routine was interrupted and he was held close by Mom as Dad drove the car. He didn't like this new ride. It was fast and scary. Flakey was taken in to the Veternarian. The man was a doctor for animals, he was nice but he poked and prodded the cat, ending the visit by giving Flakey a shot. The cat was glad to leave this place and voiced his complaint by meowing loudly. The next ride was a short one. Mom had promised the kids to bring Flakey to their class at school to show the other students. Flakey meowed in protest thinking he was going to the Vet. again.

When they brought the frightened cat into the classroom, kids surrounded him. The teacher and the Mom had the kids wait in a line to pet Flakey. He loved it, the kids were gentle and the cat purred with appreciation for all the good attention. Flakey felt special and important being the main attraction for three classes "show and tell." He was feeling loved and it was great! Flakey saw how proud and happy his kids were with his good behavior. After Flakey got home, he still didn't like the car rides, but school was a great place to visit and feel love!

Thank God for Schools!

Mary J. Brooks

Flakey's Favorite Holiday

Flakey loved the holidays, on those special days the family was around a lot more. There were other people that came to visit also. Flakey enjoyed all the extra attention. At times to many kids, made too much noise and bothered the cat with too much playing, when he wanted to just eat or sleep. Christmas time was fun for Flakey. There were ribbons, bows, wrapping, and boxes. There was a lot of good food which the cat got to sample. Some of the food was spilled, and some was sneaked to him. Valentine's day and Easter brought chocolate which was not good for the cat. The family had to be careful not to leave candy or eggs laying around where Flakey might be tempted to sample them. He was smart enough not to eat chocolate, but some pets did eat these and got very sick. They could even die!

Flakey liked the hustle and bustle in the kitchen sometimes getting under foot. Flakey liked people food, but it wasn't good for him to eat much rich food.

Flakey liked birthdays too. More ribbons and boxes. He liked hiding in boxes and playing with ribbons. Then there was the cake and ice cream. Ice Cream(without chocolate) was one of the cats favorite treats. The family gave him a little taste as milk and milk products are hard on a cats tummy.

Flakey didn't like Halloween very much. The kids would get a hold of him and dress him in doll clothes for his costume. He would sit one top of the refrigerator out of the way of the front door. The kids coming to trick and treat would get a kick out of the cat in costume. Flakey couldn't wait to get that outfit off at the end of the night!

One year as the family prepared for Thanksgiving, the turkey was put on the table and cutting board to carve. Flakey smelled the delicious smell and went under the table to see if any meat was dropping. The meat craved, my son Brad and I heard a lapping sound like a cat drinking water. They looked under the table where turkey juice was running through a crack in the table. There was Flakey lapping up the turkey juice as fast as he could. The sight was funny, but the cat was covered in greasy turkey juice. Dad captured the cat, brought him downstairs where Flakey had his first real bath. He didn't like this bath at all! He did like the turkey scraps he got later. From that time on, Flakey decided that Thanksgiving was his favorite holiday, as long as there was no bath involved. Thank God for tasty Turkey!

Mary J. Brooks

Flakey Loses A Life!

They say cats have nine life's, although that's not true. Over the years Flakey the cat came close to death many times. The family Flakey owned or thought he did, left him alone many times on weekends. Camping was no place for a cat, and Flakey didn't mind being left alone for a couple of days. If it was more than a couple days a neighbor would come in to check on, feed the cat and clean his litter box. Flakey enjoyed the run of the house, lay in on the bed in the sun and not getting disturbed. He could race around the house playing with things that were normally off limits. He would look forward to his family coming home, waiting to greet them. Although the cat acted a little made at first.

One week the family left for a vacation camping. Flakey was sad to see them leave. When he woke up later the next day he didn't feel well. He didn't feel like eating and he went down where he was first found to stay. He was in pain and couldn't tell anyone. The next day the neighbor came to check on the cat. Flakey heard him but couldn't get up because if the pain. He meowed weakly and the neighbor came downstairs, and found him very sickly. The man wrapped the cat in a towel and took him to the vet. Flakey didn't even mind seeing the Veterinarian as he knew he would get some help and relief from the pain. The vet did shaved the cats paw to put an IV in for fluids. The cat was dehydrated, then the vet. checked Flakey from end to end and found out Flakey had a blockage. Because of this the cat couldn't go to the bathroom and his system was being poisoned. After a short operation to remove the blockage Flakey was on the road to recovery. He was feeling much better and started missing his home and family. When the family came home they were surprised that their cat was missing! The neighbor came over to tell that what had happened. The whole family was thankful that the neighbor had gotten Flakey help when he needed it. They felt bad the cat had been alone, sick, and in pain. Flakey was part of their family and they dearly loved him!

The family couldn't pick him up until the next day! Mom had tears in her eyes seeing her Flakey was so skinny and stinky, but he was okay. The cat felt his family's tender, loving, care once more. He gained weight and cleaned himself well again. Everyone was happy to have Flakey back home and healing! Thank God for Veterinarians and neighbors!

Mary J. Brooks

Flakey Escapes

Even after Flakey the cat had the narrow escape outside getting stuck in the tree, he still longed to go outside. Flakey didn't understand about the dangers of the great outdoors. He would sit by the door or window looking out. The outside world held so many interesting wonders. Chirping birds flying by, buzzing bees, crawling and jumping insects, silly squirrels, and other cats and dogs walking past. Flakey was always waiting for the opportunity to get out. The cat was smart and discovered the kids went in and out of the house a lot. He followed as them to the door, and pushed on it and the door opened. Flakey laid on the steps rolling on his back enjoying the warm sunshine. Before he got too far Mom found him and brought himself inside. Flakey didn't understand why he couldn't be free. He didn't understand that the world was full of danger, it just looked interesting and exciting.

One hot summers night, the cat was feeling very restless. Flakey wanted to go out and explore. First he tried the doors which were closed tight. Then he went to each open window, he found out one of the screens was torn, so he pressed against the screen and it popped out. Flakey was able to jump out the window. Off he ran into the mysterious night. The cat spent the next few hours, chasing bugs, and exploring. Tom cat joined him and they had some fun adventures together. After awhile Tom had left, Flakey was lonesome for his family. Being the cat hadn't been away from home much, he was lost. Then he felt wet drops hitting his fur. Crack went the thunder, flash came the lightning. Poor Flakey was scared, lost, and alone. He didn't like getting wet, being outside was no longer any fun. He meowed and cried for help but no one came to rescue him. He laid to to rest under a tree out of the rain. He could see and hear really well, and he got smell even better. Using his senses he found his way home. Flakey meowed under the window. Before long Mom opened the door and called for him. He came running in the safe, security of his home. Once he was warm and dry, he cuddled up to Mom, happy to be home again. Being a naturally adventurous cat, he would get out many times over the years but now he stuck close to home. Once Flakey even got on the neighbors roof and had to be helped down. He had many scary and exciting escapades. The cat would always return, happy to be home. He would stay at home for awhile. Thank God for safe shelter!

Mary J. Brooks

Watching Flakey

There are many beautiful, fascinating sights which fill our lives. We need to stop being so busy and enjoy them before they are gone and just the memory remains. I for one love watching cats, especially Flakey the cat. As a kitten, he had so much energy, chased after anything and everything. He loved to play fight, play hide and seek with the kids, and box with paper bags. If we were busy he would chase his tail and pounce on moving toes or fingers. Now that the kids were older they were gone alot and he missed the attention they gave to him. One day a baby was brought in the house and he was curious. The baby smelled good and didn't move around much yet. As this little baby grew, she became excited to see the cat. She loved watching Flakey. Then once she pet the soft, furry cat, they both fell in love! This child was gentle, calm, and quiet. The girl was called a grandchild. Flakey was always happy see her, to feel her long silky hair and to have her tender, loving, care. She came over a lot and stayed overnight. Mom and the girl loved to watch Flakey sleep. They wondered how he could sleep so comfortable in the many strange positions. He looked content and peaceful on the hard kitchen floor laying in the sun. The cat would curl up in towels and blankets in the darkness of the linen closer. Flakey would lay on his back with his paws up in the air. He would crawl under the beds where he couldn't be reached. Then the cat sprawled out in the middle of the living room claiming attention. He was master of all and did as he pleased. Though the kichen table and counters were off limits for him.

Flakey only asked for food, water, clean litter and care. We all loved to watch him clean himself. It was especially cute when he licked his paws and cleaned his face. He would awaken me with a meow, in the morning demanding attention and love. The cats long, lithe, body would stretch out my tummy and he would purr with pleasure as I stroked him. He would jump to my lap, the sit on my shoulder when I was up and moving about the house. Flakey loved to be held like a baby, but only by me. I let him down as soon as he wanted. The cat was independent and proud. Yet dependent and unashamed to reach out for the love and care he needed. Flakey was loved and he knew it. Pets do give us unconditional love. They never hurt us by what they say. They teach us to be free and easy with the love we give. Pets never reject or remove themselves unless they are hurt or abused. We can come to our pets for comfort. They demonstrate lessons of peace and contentment. My advice is enjoy watching your pets and take time showing them love while you have them. Thank God for Pets!

Mary J Brooks

Flakey Says Goodbye

For over eighteen great years, Flakey the cat gave us lots of laughs, and alot of love! Just surviving our three little kids was a true test of how he was strong and strudy. The little girl would dress him up, the boys would wrestle and rough house with Flakey. The kids never purposely hurt the cat, but sometimes his tail or paw might get stepped on. The kids would bother him when he ate, but the cat never bit or scratched them, even when they deserved. Flakey was patient and knew Mom always would rescue him. Birds, bunnies, and boxes were his delight. He even like grocery shopping as he attacked the paper bags and got inside them to check for goodies. He would sit on his hind legs and beg for cheese, chicken, peanut butter, or any treat the family might have around. Flakey liked people and didn't hide when company came. He relished the extra attention.

After Flakey turned 15 (105 for us) his health started to decline. First he would eat a lot, then he would throw up. Eventually he stopped eating as had to be taken to the Vet. The vet checked the cat over and tested for cancer, diabetes, kidney failure and heart issues. It was a relief to discover Flakey only had an overactive thyroid. He just needed a pill a day, to take the problem away. The real trouble was getting the cat to swallow the pill. I would put the tablet part way down his throat and find it on the floor later. That smart cat would pocket the pill in his cheek and spit it out later. I finally had to crushed tablet and mixed it with his soft food. Flakey started gaining weight and feeling better. The cat was almost back to his old fiesty self. Every time I had to pick up the prescription which was at the drug store, the cashier looked at me funny when I said, "Prescription for Flakey Brooks." One girl even asked me if that was a nickname for someone. I said, "No, it's for my cat!"

The pills worked for almost three years, then Flakey began to fail. When we came home one weekend from camping he didn't greet us as usual. We found him downstairs laying in pain. He tried to walk but could only go a few steps. He looked at me as if to say, it's time to let me go. My daughter went with as I took him to the Vet. The Vet. said the best thing we could do was have him put to sleep. The vet gave us some time to say goodbye. Flakey trusted us to do what was right for him. Tears streamed down our faces as we pet the cat and showed him how much we loved him. One shot, one sigh and Flakey said goodbye. He had been a wonderful pet, and we would miss his Flakey ways. Now he was once again wild and free the way he was meant to be. Thank God for Flakey the Cat, the wonderful, wonderful cat.

Mary J. Brooks

The Sand People

I just learned a new sport, I call it Sand Sliding! We were camping near some steep sand hills one fourth of July weekend. Our grand daughter and her friend took some little girls to the sand hills.

They were dressed in old jeans and long sleeved shirts. The sand hills were hard to climb and there was no walking back down, you had to sit down and slide. The girls dropped to their seats, scooted to the edge and away they went, they had to lean back or they would roll head first down the hill. They seemed to be going a hundred miles an hour. They squealed with delight the whole way down. Up and down they went. They laid on their side and rolled, getting dizzy. They slid backwards it was fun no matter how you slide. It was starting to get dark and time to go back to the campsite. Yet, if you know little girls they wanted to stay. Our granddaughter told the girls the sand people would get them if they stayed longer. The sand people hid in the sand and came out at dark and took you into the sand to stay. The little girls said that they didn't believe in the sand people, your just making that up. Our granddaughter said okay, but I'm going back so I don't get caught. The sun started to set as the girls went down the sand. Half way down they started to scream because they felt someone grabbing at them. As they got closer to the bottom they had to fight to get loose. Just in the nick of time our granddaughter and her friend helped them fight off the sand people. They ran all the way back to the campsite, so they were safe from the sand people. Were there really sand people, or did our granddaughter and her friend grab the girls when they weren't looking?
Praise God for Smart Granddaughters.
Grandpa Duck/aka Fred Kuss

Ski Snake

When my daughter Mary and her husband Larry moved to a new neighborhood, they acquired a big group of new friends. This group had lots of fun and did many things together. Their kids joined in at times and sometimes had to stay home. When this group started going skiing together I heard all about their escapades. They even let me join them as they were open to all ages. They met me at Mount Kato for a day of skiing. That is when I found out about the ski snake. Now I always said if I fell or stumble while skiing a "snow snake" snake got me. As we all met at the top of a long hill my daughter said we should show my Dad our ski snake. The group lined up I was at the end. The first person went and stopped, the next person skied part way around the first went further and stopped, by the fifth person I got It! They were making an S like a snake as they weaved out and around each other. I really got the full experience being last of about 20. Then the first person got to go and so on until we ran out of hill. That was quite a thrill as we got better at our ski snake as the day went on.

Praise God for Fun!
Grandpa Duck/aka Fred Kuss

BIG Breakfast!!

For many years I have been hearing about Big Breakfast from my daughter, Mary. The large crowd of friends her and her husband have. Gathering and did activities with have many traditions included.

Big breakfast is just one of them. This epic event occurs only twice a year going on over thirty years now. I was invited to this event one summer when I was staying in Minnesota. I woke up early on a Saturday morning and headed to Owattona where the group camped every year. The master chef was their good friend and neighbor, but everyone brings ingredients and helps prepare the ingredients for the fry pan.

The coals were started in the Weber grill. All the helpers were chopping up bacon, sausage, and ham. Out came the biggest fry pan I had ever seen, it covered the large Weber grill. In went several pounds of bacon to fry good and crisp. Then in went the large quantities of sausage, ham, and onion. About this time my mouth started to water with the aroma, and hunger pangs began. In went the mushrooms, peppers, and hash browns. The master chef kept an eye on the mixture, using a huge spatula to turn the ingredients. The helpers are cracked about 100 eggs, 2 per person they guessed. They barely fit into the pan. Once the eggs set up, the cheese was added. The cheese is essential and four different kinds of e were added! In the meantime I snacked on some of the fresh fruit and pastries that were shared and available. The process had no taken two hours and everyone was anxiously waiting with a plate and silverware in hand. The chef announced the batch done and it was ready to eat. Heaping portions were put on our plates, some used ketchup, salsa, or tabasco. I wanted to savor every last bite which I did. After I was stuffed, we all enjoyed Marv's music(friend about my age). My grandson joined with his guitar and we all sang along. The sun was shining and it was a great day! How wonderful to be a part of Big Breakfast!!

Praise God I Am Full!

Grandpa Duck/Fred Kuss

For the first time in over forty year the Big pan was forgotten at home. Thankfully we had less people join us this time. We fried the meat in one big pan. Distributed that between another large fry pan. Split the other ingredients in the two pans, and it was just as delicious! Beacuse of the weather we chopped and prepped under the big tarp we had boughten years ago. The tarp has paid for itself many time over! Dad would have loved to see us continuing the tradition on, despite the rain. We waited a little and had Big Breakfast for lunch. One dish Dad called better than gourmet. Real down home flavor that doesn't quit and fills you up! Thank God for the memory we created with my Dad!

Mary J. Brooks

The Dogs

We first met the dogs when we went to California for my daughter Becky's wedding. Bret, her husband to be had gotten Jack at the Humane Society before he met and fell in love with Becky. Jack was huge! Imagine the big, bad, wolf in the story of "Little Red Riding Hood." Jack was the big, hyper, wolf!

He loved people and kids but scared both with his size and wild ways. He was a beautiful fellow but hard to train. They needed Jack to settle down and not be so wild. The B's as we like to call Bret and Becky, decided to adopt another dog that would be mellow and hopefully calm wild Jack down.

They found Faye at the Animal Shelter also. Faye was not a true pit bull, she was a smaller type called Staphshire terrier. Her former owner had abused Faye, and at a year old had puppies taken away from her before she finished nursing. She was thin and scrawny but the B's loved her gentle ways. The B's went to the shelter four times before they finally decided to rescue Faye and bring her home. They were a little afraid of how wild Jack, would treat gentle Faye. Jack was very happy to have a dog friend to play with and live along side. He tried to get Faye riled up, but instead over time Faye got Jack to calm down. It was a miracle but Jack though still wild at times did settle down.

When we first saw Jack we were amazed at how big and beautiful he was. Still a little crazy when there were new people near by to pet him and play. Jack didn't always realize his brute strength. Faye was a lot more reserved probably because she had been abused. Yet, she loved have attention paid to her also.

Between all the Minnesota family who came to stay for the wedding, the B's, and the dogs, things at the beach house were a little wild and crazy. Every time a dog would go by, Faye and Jack would bark like crazy. The loud barking was kind of annoying, but we all enjoyed giving them love and attention and they liked us a lot!

For the wedding pictures Becky had gotten a Hawaiian shirt for Jack to wear and Faye had on a white blouse similar to a wedding dress. They both tolerated being dressed in their wedding finery. We had to put the dogs in a back room during the wedding on the beach so their barking didn't interrupt the ceremony. It was absolutely beautiful, meaningful and emotional.

Of course right before the pictures Jack had to pee and went all over his shirt. They had to remove the shirt and then took the photos without the shirt. I think Jack did that one purpose, as he didn't like wearing a shirt!

My grand daughter who was flower girl and my daughter's friend's girls absolutely loved both Jack and Faye and were sad to leave when the time came. They knew there was a long distance between California and Minnesota, and it would be a long time if they ever saw the dogs again.

The Cat

We have had Clyde our cat for almost eight years now. He first came to us with our daughter when she moved home for a few months before heading for a new life in New York and leaving Clyde with us. At first Clyde hissed at my husband and sons, but slowly adopted us all into his life. I was overjoyed to have a cat in the house again. We had Flakey for eighteen years before we had to put him to sleep. My house didn't feel the same without a cat in it. You might say I'm a cat person. I love dogs, but not the barking, and the way they poop everywhere and one has to pick it up. Also with a dog you can't just leave them to their own devises you have to either take them along if you are going for a day, or find someone to come and take the dog out. A cat you can leave for a few days as long as you have enough a large litter box, some food out, and especially water. Cats are more independent they love you, but can live without you awhile. Dogs need your devotion, your attention and your love all the time.

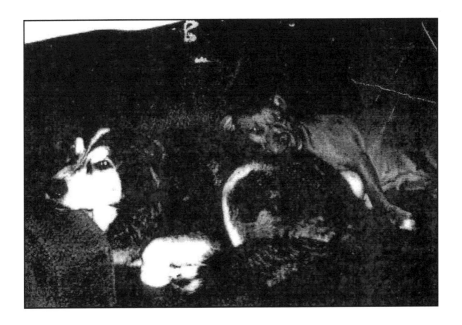

Clyde was small, black and white with a black heart shape spot on his nose. He loved to come and sit on your lap, but didn't like you to pick him up and hold him. He also loved to sneak outside, especially when it got nice out. He would almost fly out the door if anyone gave him the opportunity. We all learned to back out the door, keeping a watchful eye for our escape artist. We would forget though and out Clyde would go. He always came back though, and a lot of times he would bring his prey to share with us. Clyde owed us he ruled the house and everything in it. He walked through the house like a king and all of his subjects were privileged to come in contact with him. He loved us but needed to go where he wanted when he wanted. He was possessive of us, we were his family and he wanted us all to himself. He had tolerated my son Matt's two cats for four months when they lived here he even got to like one of them.

He was happier when they moved our and he had us all to himself again. Thank God for Dogs and cats.

Mary J Brooks

The Trip to Minnesota

We were really excited when we first found out my daughter Becky and her husband Bret, known as the B's were coming to Minnesota to start a business and live here. They left California the beginning of January. They were packed to the hilt. Bret had his car packed up and Faye was in the front seat in a doggie seatbelt, the snake Simba was in between the seats in a large plastic container. Simba is a box python about three feet long Bret had adopted her when he was volunteering at the reptile center.

All of them rode together pretty nicely and quietly except when Faye saw another dog and got excited. Becky's little car was packed leaving just enough room for Jack in the back seat. It was a very little area, for a very big dog and Jack didn't like it. By the time they made there first stop in Arizona he didn't want to get back in the car the next day. It took a lot of coaxing and a little pushing. They had a very long tiring day and at the second stop that day Jack wasn't getting back in that car. Both the B's tried but stubborn Jack let them know it was a no go. They took him and Faye for a long walk and bribed Jack with his favorite food French fries to get in the car. They were happy to get to Oklahoma and stayed an extra day to give themselves a break from driving and Jack a break from riding. Becky's uncle and family made them feel warm and welcome. The kids played with the dog's non-stop and even tired Jack out. He reluctantly got into the car for the finally part of the long journey. They were all happy and relieved to reach their final destination. Especially Jack! They couldn't get Jack near the car for awhile. It was a week before the first encounter between the dogs and our cat at our house.

The First Encounters

The first few times the dogs came with the B's to visit, we locked Clyde in the laundry room where his litter box was located. We put his food and water in with him and a nice soft blanket to lay on. He heard the dogs in his house and he was not happy. He started to yowl a mad version of a meow. Faye heard the yowl and knew a kitty cat (keecat) was in that room. She was so excited wagging her tail nose to the bottom of the door to smell that strange creature. Whap! Clyde got his paw and claws under the door and left a scratch on the top of poor Faye's nose. We had to put a long pillow in from of the door so this wouldn't happen again. After the B's and the dogs left Clyde went to every room in the house putting his scent everywhere the dogs had been. He was saying this is my house not theirs. The next time the dogs came Faye went right to the basement and the laundry room wanting to see her new friend. We were ready with the pillow in front of the door and Clyde locked away. Faye whined and Clyde yowled but they could do nothing but hear and smell each other.

The next encounter happened a few weeks later. The B's came and Clyde was upstairs to I put him in my room. My son went in to get something and put Clyde in the room across from ours. If you don't tug the door to that room all the way shut the door can be pushed open without hands. Well, you guessed it. After Faye discovered the keecat was not downstairs she went to search for him. She smelled him in the den and pushed her head to the door to get a good smell, the door opened. There was her friend, and Clyde proceeded to put a claw in her nose. Faye barked Clyde hissed, Jack was barking to protect Faye. Clyde ran into the bathroom and jumped in the tub. Both dogs knew he had gone in there but where was he? The B's both came running at the noise and got the dogs out of the bathroom as I got Clyde back in the room and shut the door tight! Poor Faye was bleeding from the claw that was removed from her nose. She had claws before from the cat where the B's were staying. One would think she would learn not to get near a cat. But Faye was obsessed and would not stay away. Thank God for excitement.

Mary J. Brooks

More Pets To Love

After being in Minnesota about three months, the B's needed to move in with us. Although I was happy and excited to have my daughter and husband with us, I wasn't quite so sure about those big dogs. The maintenance for dogs is a lot compared to cats. Poor Clyde was not happy at all. He was moved to the upstairs den and shut in for the day. At night the dogs were closed in the basement and it was Clyde's time to have reign of the upstairs. We also used a baby gate to fence off the area. Right away Faye wanted to see her friend. We were hoping the cat would get used to the dogs and tolerate them eventually. My grand daughters were ecstatic to have more pets to love at our house! Madeline now six had met the dogs in California and was excited to have them around again.

Miranda was nine and a real true animal lover. She hadn't been able to come with us out west and could hardly wait to meet Jack and Faye.

The first time the dogs came over when they were visiting they each adopted a dog for their own. Miranda took big wild Jack as she was bigger and a little calmer than Madeline. Madeline was able to handle Faye who calmed her down. Jack let the girls handle him and play, at times getting a little rough and "hugging" them. He would get up on his back to legs he would reach around their body and want to dance. "Jack, down" was heard a lot those first times. Faye loved balls one special one was like a baby to her. She would sleep with it and carry the ball around in her mouth. She liked to have people try to take it away from her. She would clamp on with her powerful jaws and growl as one tried to take it away. At first I didn't know she was playing. The girls never got tired of playing this game and Faye loved the attention. At times Jack would tease Faye by taking the ball and running off. Then Faye got upset. The first time we saw the two "play" we were concerned they were really fighting. Jack would "bite" at Faye and then put his huge mouth around Faye's head. Sometimes getting carried away Jack would leave marks on Faye. Faye would eventually get the best of Jack, she would bark and "fight" back until he gave up. Miranda and Madeline would laugh at their antics. The girls would give the dogs all the love and attention they longed for then they would go into the den and spend some time with Clyde so he wouldn't be left out. Clyde would purr happily, while the dogs would get upset and want to join the party. Thank God for love!

Walking the Dogs

One of the things I really liked about the dogs was being able to walk them. Clyde wouldn't be walked so now I had two dogs were ready and more than willing to take a walk with Gram. I was pleasantly surprised the first time I took Jack on a walk. He walked very nicely! He did have a choke collar on which helped me control him. Other dogs I've walked would pull you especially if another dog or even a person went by. When Jack saw another dog he would just whine. "Gee, I want a friend". As we walked people would stop and admire Jack. Sometimes they were afraid because of his size, but mostly in awe of his beauty. Cars would stop and ask what kind of dog he was and how old. One lady was crying because she had lost a huskie mulmute just like Jack. Parents would point out the BIG doggie to their little kids. Jack would jump up on adults because of his excitement, but he didn't jump on little ones, which was good. He didn't chase after ducks, rabbits, or squirrels. Just looked at them with interest

Faye was the opposite she wanted to go after anything that moved. Her gentle ways left her when she saw a dog, duck, rabbit or squirrel. She was fascinated by other animals and wanted to smell each and everyone. I didn't like walking her as much for she stopped at every tree, or other area that might smell like another dog or animal had been there. It took fifteen minutes to get around the block. If Faye didn't want to go she would not go. She would stubbornly smell until she was ready to go smell another place. I would always take Jack on a nice long walk first then take Faye around the block for Miss Nosy to smell what she could smell. Both Jack and Faye got in better shape not to mention me too! It was always fun and interested to walk the dogs. Where people would stop and want to pet Jack and would say how beautiful he was, they would go away from Faye afraid of her. Once in awhile some nice person would tell her how lovely she was with her smooth cinnamon coat of fur. They would even pet her and show kindness to this once mistreated animal. I always told people and kids that both dogs loved attention and were very friendly. As time went by the neighborhood got used to seeing the dogs with me and went out of their way to say Hi to them both.

Mary J. Brooks

More Encounters!

Faye grew more curious about Clyde as time went on. We decided to put the baby gate up during the day and let Clyde out as long as we were upstairs to watch. Clyde would slowly come out of the room and Faye would come running to see her friend. In fact all you had to say to Faye is "where's the keecat?" and she would come running. Jack wasn't curious about the cat. He would see Clyde and seem to say "Oh, a cat", Clyde would look at big Jack, "Oh a dog". Clyde knew that he obsessed Faye. He would leave his room wait to see Faye and sit staring at her as she whined and begged to get closer. Clyde would then go into the bathroom and look at Faye getting closer to her and teasing her. One day Clyde got right up to the gate and over he went, the dogs both had a merry chase. The rest of us almost had a heart attack. Dogs have a natural chase instinct and when something runs they chase it.

The next time Clyde got too close to the gate and the stare down took place, Faye decided she was going to see that keecat. She rammed the gate and it went down, Clyde scrambled into the bathroom with both the dogs barking on his heels. Becky screamed getting the dogs attention and Clyde hide in the tub as the dogs looked for their playmate. We quickly recovered from the near disaster and decided not to let the cat out of the room when the dogs were upstairs. That doesn't mean sneaky Clyde didn't get out again.

One day I was in the den feeding Clyde as I left with my hands full, he shot out of the room. Both dogs started barking as they took pursuit. Clyde was cornered for a moment in the hallway, hissing with his back up and ears flattened, once again Becky's scream got the dogs attention as Clyde leaped over both of the dogs and ran to hide behind the couch in the living room. The dogs quickly followed but didn't see the cat run into the kitchen. Clyde sat on the window ledge watching the dogs look for him with a superior smug look on his face. I had the B's put Faye downstairs and Jack outside as I picked up Clyde to the safe room. I felt a claw in my chest, but didn't think much of it until Becky noticed I was bleeding, Clyde had nicked a mole on me and drew some blood.

The day before this incident Jack had accidentally put a tooth in my leg. I was at my neighbors letting the dogs run around the back yard which was fenced. I was reading a didn't notice Jack took my sock which I had taken off as I enjoyed the beautiful spring day. When I was ready to go I couldn't find my sock, there was Jack with the sock in his mouth. He wanted to play with it and with me. I ignored him awhile and he put it down. I went to snatch it up and he went to grab the sock hitting me leg with his canine tooth instead. I bled a lot but luckily didn't need stitches. Earlier that winter Bret was wrestling with Jack and had to have a couple stitches by his lip as Jack got over zealous in his play. Both Jack and Faye were very strong and didn't realize their brut strength. They were very loving though and totally enjoyed the extra attention they were getting a grandpa and grams house. We all wondered what would happen next! Life in our house was always interesting now with the animals around. Thank God for all!

Mary J. Brooks

Favorite Things

One of the favorite things I liked about the dogs was the way they would greet you when you came home from some place. They would rush up to you wagging their tags, putting their noses under your hand for pets, and smile with joy. It didn't matter if you were gone a few day, hours, or even minutes. They were ecstatic to see you! One felt really loved and appreciated after being greeted by the dogs.

Jack's favorite things were food, going for a walk, and pooping. Jack would stare at you longingly whenever there was food around. He didn't jump up and try to get it though, but if you had food in your hand in his reach he would grab it. Faye's favorite things were balls of any size, going for a walk, and laying in the big chair with Gram. Balls were her babies, she would play run and fetch all day if you threw the ball. In the evenings as soon as I settled in the chair to watch T.V. Faye would run and get her ball and join me on the big chair happy to next to someone who loved her. Clyde's favorite thing was getting outside. Anytime we would leave he would watch for the chance to sneak out. As careful as we were, he was speedier. He would go for hours and come back tired and happy. Sometimes bringing home part of his prey to share with his family. This was NOT one of our favorite things!

Mary J. Brooks

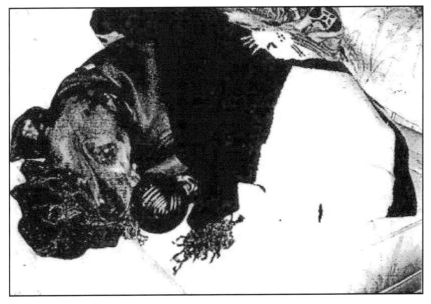

Just Playing!

The three animals played at different levels. Clyde loved plastic bags he had found a real treat in one several years ago, and has been looking for that treat again ever since. Clyde loved string, ribbon, and would at times pounce on a hand or foot being moved under something quickly. He didn't interact cat to human play like the dogs loved too play with people. The dogs were always ready and willing to play. Jack got a little to rough, not realizing his brute strength and big size. He thought he was a little dog. Faye loved her ball! She would carry this special ball around in her mouth and even sleep with the ball. If she couldn't find her special big green one, she would find another one. There were balls everywhere.

She thought of the balls as her babies. They were taken away from her, now she could mother the ball. She didn't like it when Jack would tease her and take the ball. Then there would be war, and Faye would quickly win and get the ball back, she was very quick and not mean at all. The first time the dogs really played together we were sure Jack was going to kill Faye. He would bite at her, and eventually put his mouth around her head. She would bark and give a look to Jack saying "Back off". That littler dog was solid and strong and got big, wild Jack to back off. When the dogs would start to play we would try to stay out of the way. Not intending too Jack would knock you down, or Faye would scratch you with her long toe nails.

We would also play around making the dogs look like funny humans. One night we put a wig on Jack, and he allowed It for awhile. He looked like a rock star. We put a blond wig, on cinnamon colored Faye, and then Larry and I both put on blonde wigs and we had our picture taken. What a weird family we looked like. Another evening we put Larry's glasses on Jack. He looked like a funny old man. He didn't care for the glasses look for long. Faye tolerated it just like she tolerated everything. We never lacked for quick entertainment with the dogs around.

What's that Itch

Jack and I enjoyed our walks, but at times trouble occurred without us realizing. I had taken Jack on a nice path and of course he would go to the side and pee. One of the times he got in poison ivy. He wondered why a certain part of his body was itchy and then the itch spread and was driving him crazy. He would rub his head and body in the carpet to Itch. We finally figured out he had poison ivy and the B's gave him Benadryl and a vinegar bath which greatly relieved him. I felt bad he had gotten into trouble on my watch. I felt even worse when I found out he had spread poison ivy to Faye. Becky noticed Faye's belly was beet red, and then knew Jack had spread his case to Faye, by licking her as he did periodically. You could tell right away on Faye because her coat was short and her belly rather hairless. Jack had been harder to tell because he had lots of fur everywhere! Faye got come Benadryl and a vinegar bath too. Both dogs didn't mind the bath as it relieved the nasty itch. Luckily the poison ivy case did not spread to any of us in the house. I have had poison ivy and know that it is NO fun! I'm a lot more careful when Jack goes to the side of the paths to pee now. He would do the same thing because he doesn't know any better. I warn him "don't go to far in the weeds or you'll get the itch again" he just looks at me like "Huh? Let's get walking!" So far we've kept tick free and itch free. Jack has found some dead birds and put them in his mouth, but drops them after he discovers they are dead. Nothing to play with here he thinks. He did find some baby rabbits at my friend's house and if they were alive before he put them in his mouth, they were gone by the time he "played" with them. I wasn't about to try to take them away. Jack might be a nice dog, but he is an animal and has SHARP canine teeth. One never knows and has to respect animals and their wild instincts. Jack is part wolf as well as a domesticated dog. Any animal can turn on humans so be wise, and careful despite the size. Treat animals kindly and they will be kind, and loving to you. Thank God for kindness!

Mary J. Brooks

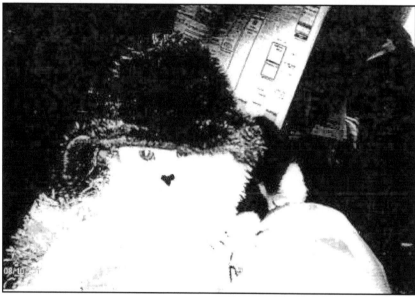

The Attack

Shortly after the dogs settled in our house, we realized our cat Clyde was not happy having two big dogs coming into his home. His freedom became limited during the day, as he was in the den. At night he could roam, while the dogs were limited to the basement. We put a baby gate up so the dogs especially Faye couldn't get to the cat. More than once Faye saw the cat and tried to get closer causing havoc.

One day the door was left ajar, there was Faye and out came Clyde, the chase was on. The cat was faster, getting into small places and hiding as the dogs barked and hunted for the cat. Becky came and got Faye downstairs as she was overly excited seeing the cat. Jack, sat innocently in the living room wondering what all the fuss was about. All of a sudden out comes Clyde jumping directly on Jack's back, claws and All! Now Jack has a heavy, furry, husky coat, and probably didn't feel much of the cats needle like claws. Yet that little cat scared that big brute of a dog. From then on, when Jack came upstairs to go out, he checked to make sure that attack cat was not nearby. A ninety pound huskey, mulmute wolf dog, was no match for a eight pound cat with claws!

The Runaway

The dogs were with us for a year, and we got into a new routine. When the winter came Jack absolutely loved the snow. When my husband snowblew the driveway Jack jumped to be blasted by the snow. When he wanted to rest he would bury himself in the snow. I didn't take as many walks due to ice, but I would still walk the dogs for a short distance. Jack was so excited to walk in the snow he kept pulling me with him. Usually he walked better, as he pulled his choke collar came undone and he was free. He took off like a streak running wildly through the deep snow. I was scared he would get hit by a car or lost amoung the streets of our neighborhood. There was no way I could keep up with him. I called his name and listened for his loud bark. Sure enough Jack had stopped by a fenced in yard to greet the dog that was outside there. I got him back in his collar and was thankful to get Jack home in one piece. The next time I took him, I put some treats in my pocket. There was one thing Jack liked more than walks, it was doggie treats. Once again the dogs collar slipped off, but I got the treats out before he took off. I hooked him up again and then I saw the area of the collar that was bent and slipping off. We headed back home where I had his owner fix the problem. When we took our granddaughter sledding Jack pulled the sled with the girls on it through the snow with no problem. We would get some strange looks as we came back full of snow from the hill a couple blocks away. Faye went to but didn't like the snow as much as Jack. Her coat was not as thick and furry, her type dog was not made for the snow and cold. She liked being covered by blankets next to someone who would pet her. Thank god for warmth!

Mary J. Brooks

Water Hate Water Love!

Another thing that dogs love that cats don't is water. Clyde does not like to get wet! He likes to drink water but not from a dish or cup but directly from the faucet. One night he leaped onto the toilet to get on the counter with the sink in the bathroom. My husband who is a culprit of leaving the seat up had left up, the toilet lid, well the slippery lid was too much for Clyde. His back end went splash in the clean toilet water. He leaped up and out the bathroom so fast I didn't even see what happened. I laughed when I saw him licking his hindquarters, and shaking himself in disgust. He wasn't happy at his almost bath in the toilet!

I myself love the water and couldn't wait to see how the dogs acted when we went to the beach for the first time. Jack went splashing in with wild abandonment, where Faye was cautious at first and then very playful.

I had Jack on his walking leash and we run in the water enjoying the coolness. It was a hot July day and soon we went deeper out Jack was swimming and loving every minute. He saw me and tried to climb on me, but I swam away as not to have this ninety-pound dog drowned me. He got tired and headed for shore taking me with him. We got out and Jack immediately rolled in the sand. I tied him to the chair as I went out for a longer swim. Jack didn't like seeing me way out in the water, and decided to come back in chaise lounge and all! We laughed at his helpfulness as I wanted to lie in the water but not quite that far out.

Faye loved running and playing in the water, but she didn't want to swim. I tried several times but she stubbornly refused. She was friskier than usual instigating play with Jack where Jack usually teased her into "playing". We had a couple hours of fun, and I will never forget Jack and Faye at play in the water we all love.

Mary J. Brooks

Simbu Sheds His Skin

Now you've heard a lot about the dogs that came to live with us, and the cat that "owns" us, but I have neglected "Simbu". He is the quiet member the household, a beautiful snake called a box python. He is about three feet long with a diamond like pattern running down his slick body. One might think the snakes are slimy, but they are not, they feel smooth but a little course. Simbu doesn't bark, or run wild like the other animals. He is content to curl up in a circle and sleep under his "rock". The rock is heated with a hole craved into the bottom where Simbu can enjoy warm, darkness and peace and quiet. Once in a while Simbu comes out to "smell" something interesting, or to eat. About once a month he eats a "sleeping rat", a rat that has been put to sleep for his dinner. One time the pet store where Bret gets the rat didn't put it to sleep. Bret didn't know what to do, as he didn't want to be the one to kill it. He tried putting it in with Simbu, but the snake and the rat just stared at each other. Finally Bret had to take it out and bonk it on the head. Conditions have to be just right for stubborn Simbu to eat. He doesn't like a lot of noise or people around. In the winter he hibernates and doesn't eat for about four months. Our grand daughter Madeline had held him, she is fascinated by the snake and loves watching him.

Bret and Becky brought Simbu, to school on snake week. The small children loved him, petted him and listened with fascination to the information Bret told them. Pictures were taken and Simbu was the star of the day, although he didn't really enjoy the spotlight.

As the summer began Simbu came out from his rock and started to itch himself. Eventually he shed his skin the entire length of his body came off in on long piece. We are saving this to show the kids when school starts again. They will be interested to see Simbu's skin and he doesn't mind sharing that with anyone.

Maybe he'll come back to school again, but now in the summer he lays on top his rock and enjoys the lazy, hazy, crazy, days of summer. He loves the heat and hates the cold winters.

Most of us love Simbu and his quiet, gentle, ways. Some people are scared of snakes and would rather not see them.

But Simbu would never hurt anyone he just minds his own business. Thank God even for snakes!

Mary J. Brooks

Dogs Gone

I was excited about having my daughter and her husband move it with us for awhile. I wasn't to excited excited to have two big dogs come and stay with us. Jack, was a husky, mulmute/wolf dog weighing about ninety pounds about seventy pounds was fur! Faye was smaller and not furry, but still took up a lot of space and had long claws that would tear furniture material. We covered the couch and chairs, and continually swept and vacumned. I enjoyed walking with the dogs, and cuddling with them. Faye sat next to me in my big chair as I watched T.V. Jack got too hot and laid on the floor by us. The longer the dogs stayed with us the more I grew to love those two rascals. I didn't like picking up their poop, or listening to their loud barks as dogs or people walked by. The neighborhood got to know the dogs and greeted them with treats and pets. When my daughter and her husband went to visit New York City we were in charge. As grandparents do, we spoiled our grand Dogs! When their owners came back the dogs just wanted to be by me and my husband. My daughter and her husband decided to look for chef jobs and move to NYC. They both loved it there! Our time with our grand dogs was coming to an end. Two months later they packed up. Bret went first, found a place to live, and started his job as executive chef. Then my husband drove with Becky to help her with the dogs and driving. There was no room for Simbu(their snake and his tank) He stayed with us another three months. We were all sad to see our dog friends leave, and of course the B's leave too. It was an exciting new adventure for all of them. We would visit once they were settled in their new place and new jobs.

A Simbu Scare

Most of our friends thought we were crazy to let a snake stay in our basement. Simbu had a large fish tank which he lived in and had never escaped. The snake was also very quiet and shy. He mostly stayed under the rock in his tank curled up for warmth and sleep. Every once in a while he would come out to look for food. The one part I didn't like is having to go buy a frozen rat for his monthly meal. One had to let it thaw and then tossing the rat in by the snake for his meal. Simbu didn't like you watching him start his meal. But once he swallowed it whole you could watch to travel down his body. He left one rat alone because I put it in tail first. The snake would only eat the rat head first. That was a wasted meal and wasted money. From then on I put the rat in correctly!

One night I heard a noise downstairs. I went to check it out without putting on my glasses. It wasn't my son who slept downstairs now. I stopped frozen at the bottom of the stairs. There was Simbu laying on the floor by his tank. I didn't want to pick him up with my bare hands, so I got a broom. I thought maybe he would wind around it as box pythons wind around prey. Then I saw movement in the tank, and there was the snake. I walked closer to the object I thought was the snake. It was my son's long dark belt. What a relief that was for me! When my daughter came back to get the rest of her stuff and the snake, I put on gloves and picked up Simbu moving him the a smaller abode until the got back to Brooklyn where they now lived. Both Faye and Jack are gone now, as all dogs(and pets) go to heaven. Yet Simbu remains in his tank almost 30 years old. The snake had several close calls like getting out going under the bed where my grand daughter was staying and trying to digest her short. Thankful the snake was discovered and saved! What a ruckus this incident caused at 2 am. Thank God for Grand Snakes, and Grand Dogs!!!

Mary J. Brooks

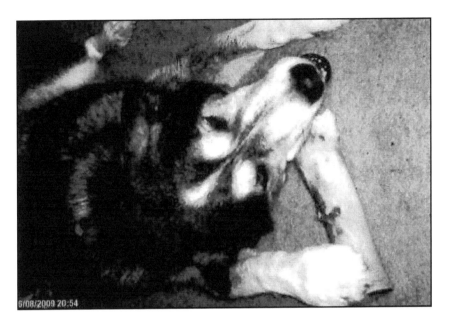

Caring for Clyde

My daughter Becky had moved out on her own. The first chance she got she rescued her first pet. She didn't know Clyde's past story, just that he needed a home and someone to care for him. Clyde was used to being out on his own. Yet he was stray that like people but loved to be outside like feral cat. By the time my daughter saved him from the shelter he had come close to using up his supposedly nine lives. Clyde was black and white with a black heart shape pattern on his nose. Becky lived in a big house with lots of other people. Some she knew others she didn't. Everyone had there own room and Clyde had the run of the place. If house mates left their rooms open Clyde would go investigate. He came upon some weed like stuff in a plastic bag, that made him feel good like cat nip did. Later after Becky moved again, she lived on her own. She was right on a busy street in north Minneapolis. The neighbors all knew Clyde because he kept escaping. Becky left for a week and her brother Matt was taking care of Clyde. The second time Matt stopped to check on the cat, Clyde had torn the screen of a partially open window and escaped, roaming the busy streets. We didn't mention this to Becky when she called in hopes that Clyde would come back. A few days later Matt walked around the area looking for Clyde, got the mail and let himself in Becky's place. Matt was shocked to see Clyde back in the apartment. Becky's neighbors had seen Clyde and caught him. The landlord put the cat back in the apartment, and boarded up the window.

Awhile later Becky moved back home a few months and brought Clyde with her. Clyde didn't know us very well and hissed at my husband and son, when he joined our household. Once more I could show my tender love and care to a cute, cuddley, creature. By the time Becky left for a new life in New York, Clyde had adopted us. He filled up the empty space left by Flakey, but he wasn't as laid back as Flakey had been. Caring for Clyde came naturally to me. He pawed his way into our hearts and lives. We would give him the tender, loving, care every cat so richly deserves. We noticed his fetish for plastic bags, and heard the story of why he licked, pawed, and smelled them. He also investigated paper bags as Flakey had done. At night Clyde would come into our room and paw my face, it was like he said "Pet Me!" NOW! I would give in and pet him, but eventually put him out of the bedroom and close the door, so I could get some sleep. Early mornings Clyde would sit on Larry's lap to get some petting. Clyde would tolerate the teasing and play with my son, Brad. He would call the cat silly names, and together they would play funny games. Yet, when Brad was feeling depressed and to sad to move, Clyde would lay on his chest, warming the human with the cats love and purring. Cats seem to sense feelings of the people they live around. Pets are protective and Clyde would help us feel better when we needed. Thank God for giving us comfort.

Mary J. Brooks

Clyde's Call of the Wild

We loved our adopted cat. He was gentle and mild, then crazy and wild. One thing we didn't like was Clyde's zest for the outside world. The minute anyone would meander out the door, the cat would zoom outside. Clyde was supposed to be an indoor cat, but he had gotten used to exploring the great outdoors. We had to back out the door and watch for him so he didn't get out. We even put a sign on the door for when we had visitors. Then we would forget and a visitor didn't know what the sign meant and all one would see was a flash of black and white. "What was that", they would say and we told them about our runaway!

When Clyde got out he would be gone for hours, and I would get nervous about his safety. When the cat would return he meowed by my window so I would let him inside. We lived in the suburbs but had a com field across the street in back of the houses there. We also had trails and a park reserve with all kinds of wild life. We would see fox, coyote, deer, and even bear had been spotted near by. Clyde would return home with a treasure to give us, dropping a dead mouse, rabbit, or bird at our door. My husband told Clyde to get all the rabbits and mice the cat wanted but leave the birds alone. We had heard an owl in the tree nearby, and my husband even saw him. One night after an putting Clyde came home with a long scratch under his fur. We think the owl almost got Clyde, but the cat got away. It would be interesting to have a camera with Clyde as he investigated at night. My neighbors liked to see him out hunting for vermin and keeping them away from our houses!

One night we were having a campfire in the backyard, Clyde got outside and ran to the field. Later on he had gotten back in the house and left his offering on the living room carpet, dead and without a head. There was blood on my carpet, I took some newspaper and picked the animal up and out throwing it away. Quickly I cleaned it up before my little grand daughter saw the animal, what ever it was. We think maybe a mole. Before long the call of the wild came again. My Dad and Mom were staying with us for the summer. Clyde saw them as people to get treats from, and a good way to get out the door. Clyde got out and was out chasing all night. At four in the morning we heard this loud cry, almost like a loud baby.

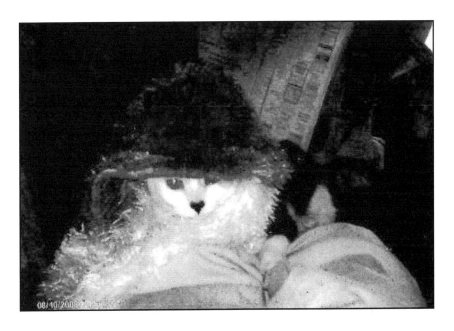

I woke up and remembered Clyde was still outside. Then I heard Clyde meowing loudly. I went to the door and the cat pranced inside. He glanced back and then I saw a small coyote in our front yard by the far tree. Clyde seemed unafraid like he didn't have a care in the world. The coyote cried again, mad that he had just lost his breakfast. My Dad and Mom heard the cry and asked about it the next morning. My Dad writes stories too and said that was a good story! We had Clyde for over twelve years and though we were more careful, the cat answered the call of the wild many times. He got out before he got sick, and was locked in someone's garage for three days. We thought he was gone forever. He started getting thin and throwing up his food.

The Vet thought he might have gotten poisoned or maybe had cancer. There was nothing we could do for him, though he wasn't in pain. After a week I decided to bring him in like we did Flakey, Clyde also asked to be let go with his eyes pleading, he now was in pain and ready to go. The next morning I found him on the basement tile gone forever. We had a service for Clyde and buried him by the garden where he used to explore. Now he was free, frolicking with all of God's creatures gone before our dear, well loved Clyde! Thank God for his creatures!

Mary J. Brooks

Ruth Dog

Jack the big husky, mulmute, wolf was so sad after Faye died. He laid around looking sorrowful. When a dog would go by he would get excited until he saw it wasn't Faye. Faye had been so gentle and sweet with humans. Yet she had whipped Jack into shape and taught him about being a dog. It wasn't long before the B's decided they needed another dog for Jack and for them. They started looking at shelters, and of course needed Jack's approval. She was scrawny, and smelly, not shy though. The dog at the shelter picked them, and Jack okayed her. They named her Ruth, which was Becky's grandma's name. Ruth dog had pretty chocolate colored markings on her white coat. Her face was so expressive she could have been a dog model. Yet, Ruth was rambunctious, nothing at all like her name sake. Jack had to teach her how to settle down and be a part of the family. Ruth Dog had been starved, beaten, caged, and unloved. She also had had puppies as part of a puppy mill, cruel, inhuman place to be. Now she was fixated on food and attention. She also enjoyed walks, but was slow and nosy just like Faye. Jack liked Ruth, and wasn't as lonely. Ruth loved Jack and followed his lead. Ruth would jump on people and want pet and attention anyway she could get it. She was built like a ton of bricks as shaffordshire terrier usually will be. When she liked you she would jump on your leg and get excited. It was very hard to stop her. She had long thick nails that were almost impossible to trim, one could get scratched badly by accident. Ruth wouldn't hurt anybody purposely unless you hurt her owners. She had the loudest bark and it wasn't pleasant to hear. She was ready to play, to walk, to nap, or to eat, at all times! She was living the best life, then some things happened. Jack left home after crossing the rainbow bridge to pet heaven. Ruth missed her friend and family member. She laid around the house looking confused and sad.

To make matters worse her owners brought home some blankets and baby clothes and she smelled a new interesting smell. Next they brought home a little human that smelled the same. Ruth was cautious but curious. This little human just laid around, sometimes it would cry. Ruth didn't like that sound, it worried her. This little boy grew fast and Ruth liked him when he started eating at the table. He would spill and she would get the scraps. As the boy got bigger he would give Ruth food he didn't want, but didn't like it when Ruth Dog took his favorite food. This boy was always busy, running, and jumping, and playing with balls, and toys. He was always making noise. Ruth liked it when he would settle down and cuddle up by her. One day the little boy left and the dog didn't see him all day. Where was his boy? Was he okay? Later the little boy came back and Ruth kept her eye on him the rest of the night. From then on the boy was gone alot, but always came back. Ruth loved her boy now part of her family. She was getting old and needed more rest and quiet now. Ruth was loved and cared for having the best life after a real rough start. Thank God for rescue!

Mary J. Brooks

The Great Unsung Race

My daughter, Mary calls me every day, which I look forward too. She always has a story to tell. The crowd of friends she hangs out with, always is doing something fun. They went to the horse races together. They liked watching the dog races. It had become a custom to go and bet on the greyhounds. This was one of their traditions that was hard to break. When the dog tracks closed nearby they decided to hold their own race. Not dogs, not horses or pigs, but minnows. Yes minnows! These unsung races will go down in history in the annals of sporting events. Emotions run at a fever pitch as everyone picks out what they think is the fastest minnow. Bets are made, individuals are pitted against one another. The suspense can be cut with a knife. Two long narrow gutters are taped together, water is added but not too high to avoid spillage. About 30 people are packed into a large party room. Before the races begin there is tailgating and snacks galore. The first racers are ready in the water filled styrofoam cups. There is red tape near the end of the track to mark the finish. On your mark, get set, go. The minnows are poured into their tracks. The track is a straight line, but the minnows get stubbon, go the wrong way or stop all together. The crowd is going wild, yelling encouragement, and shouting hurrah as the winner reaches the finish. The races continue until all have participated. Then the losers race losers, and winners race winners until we have the minnow champion and their owner. There is prize money for first, second, and third place. The biggest loser needs to deal with the minnows and some good natured kidding. I never got to go watch these unsung races, but I enjoyed hearing about them.

Praise God for Good times. Grandpa Duck/aka Fred Kiss

Campfires

One thing I have always enjoyed is a blazing campfire. Our family loved to camp and the fire we started at the end of the day was our favorite part. We would roast hotdogs, marshmallows, make hobo pies, or smores. We would tell spooky and silly stories, and of course sing songs. Everyone had their favorite song and we sang them all. My favorite besides the hymns, was "I've been working on the Railroad." When I was young my brother Jerry and I would walk to the rail yard nearby and play. We weren't suppose to play there, but we were fascinated by the big trains. We had a few close calls, and could have been badly hurt. My dad found out before anything really bad happened. We had our fanny's tared and stopped going where we weren't aloud. Yet, the memory of those good old days and the adventures I had with my brother always remained. When we visited my daughter, Mary or my son Dan, we had fires in a pit or moveable fireplace outside in the yard. It was nice to feel the warmth on a cool Minnesota evening. One could also feel the warmth of one another as we gathered together and shared stories and songs.

Praise God for Campfires!
Grandpa Duck/aka Fred Kuss

Horse Tales

Around eight years old, I started being horse crazy. The neighbors behind us had started breeding and raising horses on some land in the country. They invited us out to see and even ride the horses. From the moment I first rode on a horse, ! fell in love with both horses and riding. We got to go out a couple times before both of our families moved. One time ! had my turn and was waiting and hoping for a second turn. My little brother Dan, came by the horse I was petting and started bugging the horse. I told him to stop, but by then the horse was mad and reach around and bit me in the leg. I wasn't mad at the horse, he was protecting himself. I was mad at my brother, and my leg was black and blue for weeks. I used to watch National Velvet, a tv show about a girl and a horse. I would pretend my bike was a horse and I was jumping. When I got older and moved to the city, my two best friends were horse crazy also. We would walk or bike to go riding at stables miles away. It was expensive but I used all my baby-sitting money to be able to go riding. Then I met a boy who had a horse, and others that had horses nearby. I was asked to go riding, and even though the guy was only a friend I accepted dates to ride. One afternoon we were in town and the guy did a trick where the horse I was on would rear up. I held on but once the horse came down I lost my grip and fell off. I hit the sidewalk with my chin, somehow not injuring myself more. That was the last time I dated the guy and rode his horse. He thought it was funny, especially when my chin looked like I had a beard.

Years later my friend gave me a trail ride on a horse for my birthday. We were in the Black Hills, and it was quite an experience going up the hills on the narrow trails. At the top we were able to trot and cantor for awhile. What beauty surrounded us as we savored the wonder of nature. The last time I rode we were camping and a group of friends went for a trail ride. We climbed up on platforms and were helped up on the horse. My horse kept wanting to trot, and it made me laugh. My friend wanted to but her horse didn't want to trot. Trotting is pretty bumpy, cancoring is my favorite which my horse did at the end of the trail and I loved it. Getting off was difficult and funny at the same time. My legs were pretty shaky after. I have one more wish while I still can. To ride on a beach with my horse in a cantor for as long as ! like. Thank God for Horses to ride and enjoy!

Mary J. Brooks

Raccoon Robbers!

One must admit they are kind of cute with those masks always on their face. Yet with their fingerlike hands they can open locked items and take items that attract them. We camped with friends that warned us about raccoon robbers. They had a grill with a grease pan attached and we had gotten one just like it. They left it out one night and the grease pan was gone the next day, raccoons love grease.

We made sure to put our grease pan away after that story. One night their was a baby raccoon at our campsite. Though it was small it got too close for comfort. My son and his daughter ran to climbed on top of the picnic table. Then the raccoon ran behind one of the trailers. Where did he go? He got in the crawl space between the floor and one of the campers. My sister in law was worried about the creature getting in to her at night. I teased her that during the night he would curl up on her head like a fur hat and sleep without her knowing the raccoon was there. Then it would move and she would wake up screaming and chasing the animal out. I liked teasing at times. Knowing that raccoons liked grease we took leftover sausage broke it into pieces and made a trail of treats to get the raccoon out. The next day the raccoon was gone and so were the treats. My sister in law didn't have a raccoon hat either!

We went camping with our grandkids a couple times a year. I was in charge of meals one day, and my sister in law was in charge of the other day the kids helped. I had made a delicious pot roast and the next day my sister in law was making spaghetti and meatballs. It was time to put the meatballs in but they were no where to be found. We looked everywhere, then my husband found an empty big plastic zip lock bag. The meatballs had been in the cooler in the zip lock bag. Those robber raccoons had stolen our meatballs. Boy was my sister in law mad, if she saw a raccoon she would have turned them into a meatball or a hat! Instead we used the leftover roast which made the spaghetti even more delicious and we didn't share with one raccoon! Thank God for Raccoon Robbers and leftovers.

Mary J. Brooks

Coyote

Every year we would camp at the same place in the fall with many of our friends. When it got dark it was a little scary especially when no other campers were around. We would always build a roaring fire for both warmth and protection from any wild animals near by. Deer, bear, porcupine, and skunk has all been spotted on our travels through the area and we didn't want to run into anyone of these. Late one night we were sitting enjoying the fire when we heard a chorus of coyote just over the hill chasing prey in the field. We all stopped talking, got up, and moved as close to the fire as we could. We listened to the chase and it seemed like any minute those coyote would come up the hill to us. In all the years we camped at this place we had never had this happen. We were pretty shaken up, but stayed safely by the bright fire. This happened a few other times over the years, so we always stayed together when we walked somewhere. We always built a huge fire to keep those coyote and other animals at bay! Thank God for Fire!

Where Do The Buffalo Roam

We have had many wild and wonderful adventures on our travels over the years. When we went on a camping trip to South Dakota with two other couples, we were going to see all we could see. Once we got to our campsite near Hill City and Mount Rushmore we made a plan. We were all excited to travel to Custer State Park. Our mission, was to get close enough to the wild buffalo to be amazed. I had seen some long ago, but wanted a closer view this time. We traveled through the park and got out of the car viewing buffalo far away. We took uncharted roads and looked for buffalo roaming close by. Where did the Buffalo roam? We finally atopped at the visitors center and asked. Other people were there too and looked at us strangely. The guy at the desk said turn left at the next road and you will find some buffalo. We did and there they were many, many buffalo on the road, by the road, next to our car. We took pictures and waited our turn. We didn't think or feed these big beast like some silly, stupid people. These animals were huge and should be respected and feared. Some shook the earth when they sat down.

07/26/2005

We could see the many swallows they made from their resting places. There were mom's and babies, and giant dad's with beautiful shaggy brown fur. I got a little emotional seeing a piece of America's past still roaming free, but needing to be protected from mean and mangy people. I wonder if the Buffalo will still be roaming for my grandchildren to see. Thank God for beautiful Buffalo?

Mary J. Brooks

Grand Cats, Grand dogs, Grand Birds,

Over the years I have enjoyed the many pets my kids have attained. My oldest grand daughter is especially an animal lover. First she had a cute little lop ear bunny. Then a puppy with very long legs who loved to jump. Miranda also had a set of lovebirds that were very pretty. They had to be covered at night not to make noise. Once Miranda moved out on her own she was able to get the animals she really wanted cats. First came Dewey, then Phoebe, now she added Winston. I now call her the Cat lady!

Madeline just got two kittens, Bins and Milo so cute and cuddley. Curious and crazy too! Then we have Henry and Thomas who live with my grandsons William and Jacob and there parents. The B's still have Simbu the snake and Ruth. We make the most of time with each on of them and enjoy giving extra love and attention as all grandparents do. Now that I have my own cat I am extra joyful! Thankful for being Grandma!

Cece: Care Cat

One of the best surprise gifts I ever received was my care cat. I have always loved cats and hadn't had one in many years. My husband said, "No more pets." His word is usually law around our house. My grand daughters tried to persuade him, but I knew better. I was sitting in my recliner, reading after my third same hip replacement surgery due to ongoing infection. I was feeling kind of down and out after over a year of set backs.

There was my husband with a small cat carrier in his hands, there was a beautiful little cat inside. I asked "Who's is that?" He said, "She's yours!" He took the cat out and sat her on my lap, where she laid for hours enjoying my attention and love. She was scared and scrawny, but had beautiful soft fur and markings. I especially loved the M on her forehead, meaning Maine coon. Her name had been Sissy, but I didn't care for that. She was now My care cat, cosy cat, comfort cat, so Cece fit her wonderfully!

She fit into our life purrfectly! She loved food and gets special treatsmthree times a day. I think she might have been deprived at the other house she lived,in with cats, dogs, and an older lady. Cece always wanted me to go downstairs where her food was and watch her eat. I think to make sure no other animal got her food. She sits and stares stares at us when we eat. Putting her paws, but not claws on my leg. I of course spoil her and give her a few pieces of whatever we are having. Sometimes I have to put her down the basement because she bothers me too much. Her favorite place to me is on my lap, which I love. Cece loved her routine and didn't like when change came along. When I'm out of my chair, she lays there. She does go to my husband once in awhile too. She likes to play with balls, string, grapes, pill covers, anything that rolls, and away she goes. At night she lays at the foot of my bed, then will come and lay on my chest, licking my chin, She will lay by my head, and then under the covers to be right next to me. I'm her person, and she is my little love! Cece likes other people and doesn't hide when company comes. She loves being petted, but doesn't like being picked up and held. She was afraid of my grandsons at first, but they are okay when they quiet down and just gently pet her. Quiet is what she likes, she also has the quietest meow ever. I like that! Cece is a scaredy cat. The first thunder storm we head, she ran to the basement steps and hid. She wouldn't even come to me, just laid there until no storm was over. She also doesn't like the lawn mower, the vacumn cleaner, or any loud noises. I had never seen this with any of my other cats. Cece doesn't like it when we leave her alone for a few days. Unlike my other cats, she doesn't get mad, she rubs my legs with her body, and follows me everywhere for a few days.

Elm Creek Animal Hospital
(763) 427-5150

We bought her two cat trees, the one upstairs had a perch but she was a little scared of this. Once I started putting her treats there, she started loving it. Cece sits there near the big window watching birds, squirrels, dogs, and people going by. She loves to lay in the sun and nap away from anyone that might bother her. This was her safe place, besides laying on my lap. We watch TV and the cat is interested in the animals she sees. This silly cat loves to drink from the bathroom sink faucet. Our other cats did this, but Cece never misses an opportunity to jump up,and have us turn the water on lightly.

Cece is the cleanest cat ever! She is constantly grooming and washing herself. Her fur is long and she has a lion like mane under her head, pure white. At times her fur gets matted, so I brush her more now. She loves to be brushed but doesn't like having her claws clipped. It doesn't hurt, and when my son holds her she puts up with it. My other son comes and cares for her when we are gone. Cece really likes both of them! We keep Cece inside, although she is getting used to the gazebo but she scares easily. The cat is much happier when we are together. Whether we play, or rest, watch TV, or snuggle together, we love each other and share this great feeling whenever we can. Giving love, and showing love is the best gift of all! Thank God for Cece, my care cat!

Mary J. Brooks

New York Adventure

We all missed the B's and the dogs after they moved to Brooklyn, New York. After they were settled in New York a few years my son, his wife and three kids decided to drive out to see them. We were invited also, and took the long drive out there without stopping for the night. The kids had movies playing and tablets for games. The big van helped separate them from the "he touched me" complaints. We went through Manhattan around 2 am. It was so lit up it seemed like day. After taking a few wrong turns, we made it. The next day I stayed home due to dizziness. The others did some sight seeing near by. The next day we hung around. I took Jack, who was now a blind dog, on a walk. This seeing eye human, had to get used to steering him around obstacles. I accidentally bumped him into a garbage can and he got a bruise on his nose. Sorry, Jack! I was more careful after that incident. Michelle, Madeline, and I played a new card game. Down below us was the snakes cage. Unknowingly Michelle accidentally opened it up with her foot. Later we took the subway into to see the city. Rockefeller Center, Time Square, Broadway, M & M store, etc. Every time we rode the Subway the voice cautioned, "Please stand clear of the closing door." Then a ding ding sound. Little Jacob loved it, and started repeating the voice. William was enthralled by the whole experience.

We got back at 2:00 am. We were all getting ready for bed when Madeline screamed and said there was a snake under her bed downstairs. We woke up Bret, and he rescued Simbu, the box python from eating Madeline's shorts. There was quite an outburst from the downstairs group. Simbu wouldn't purposefully hurt anyone but with the little ones sleeping on sleeping bags, one could't be to careful! We had other adventures going to ride the Statin Island Ferry, seeing the Statue of Liberty, the Freedom Tower, 911 Fountains and Memorial, Wall Street, Central Park, Grand Central Station, and getting lost on the way back to Becky and Bret's. It was really fun people watching too! We were sad to say goodbye. We did make a stop to sleep on the way back to Minnesota. Thank God for Adventures!

Mary J. Brooks

Comfort Creatures

Throughout our life on Earth we receive comfort and care from God's great and glorious creatures. Humans and animals alike enrich and energize our existence. From beautiful birds we enjoy daily, to the animals we see scurry about outside. Creatures that entertain us with their antics. Then there are animals that we see in the woods, the water, and wetland. We can appreciate watching these interesting creatures.

Next are the animals that we see at the zoo, at a theme park, or on a safari! We might have the surprise of seeing creatures in the sea, on a mountain, in the forest, or maybe crossing the road. These sighting are a gift to us for a brief moment of time.

Then we have a precious, playful, perfectly loved and longed for pets. We care for them, they comfort and care for us. These creatures bring us joy, laughter, and love. Many times we have to say goodbye, followed by a sorrow filled cry. Magical memories always remain!

Our first creatures of comfort and concern are our human gifts, our parents, our protectors. We learn pure passion from their arms, their voice, their examples of love and loyalty. We might also be able to experience the sweetness of sharing with siblings. These creatures that we grow along side and make a history unlike any other in our lives. We are given relatives to enhance our time here on Earth, further gifts of generous and gentle devotion. Friends of our choosing fill our lives with fun, faithfulness, and future hopes and dreams. Creatures whos gifts are fill us with lauggter, loyalty and love. Precious creatures who care for us and share their lives with us. People we can lean on, when things go wrong. People who surround us with support and help us be strong. Priceless people who make life worth living by giving us their heart and soul. Their unending, forgiving, amazing, beautiful, forever love.

Thank You God for all creatures of comfort!
Mary J Brooks